BLUE FOOD

A collection of fun, diverse original monologues perfect for beginning acting classes and auditions.

Sixty-six monologues for actors from 16 to 96.

And...

Did You Kiss Me?

A collection of sixteen new formless scenes!

By Janice Fronczak

PUBLISHED BY

DOMINION PUBLICATIONS

888-350-5005

Rights for the plays in this anthology may be
obtained by calling Dominion Publications at:
1-888-350-5005.

Dominion Publications
PO Box 248
Cedar Rapids, IA 52406

ISBN: 978-1-61588-201-4

*I dedicate **Blue Food** to my mother, all of my ancestors from Galveston, my supportive and wise husband, Jef, and my two wonderful sons, Nathan and Gabriel.*

—Janice Fronczak

TABLE OF CONTENTS

PART TWO: MALE MONOLOGUES

PART THREE: SENIOR MONOLOGUES

FOR FEMALES:

FOR MALES:

PART FOUR: NEBRASKA-INSPIRED MONOLOGUES

FOR FEMALES:

FOR MALES:

PART FIVE: ALASKA-INSPIRED MONOLOGUES

PART SIX: FORMLESS SCENES

**Senior monologues

PART ONE:
FEMALE MONOLOGUES

THE ACTRESS

AUTHOR'S NOTE:
This was the first monologue that I ever wrote. It turned out to be a very funny quirky female character. This particular monologue has won many young actresses roles in community theatres as well as in summer stock. She's one of my favorites. Don't pull away from the physical choices here!

A self-absorbed young actress explains her journey to becoming a "deep" actress.

It's not that I don't like her. I mean...she's a good actress...well...she's okay. It's not that I think I'm better than anybody else. It's just that...I'm better than anybody else! I take the stage. I'm not wish-washy, ramsy-pansy about it. I claim it for mine own. And I go deep. I'm a very deep person. I am very deep. I'm so multi-leveled, that sometimes I cry. NO! - - I WEEP. Do you know what I'm saying? Are you deep like that? I have felt that you're deep. It's something to look into. I'm going to tell you something and you must swear not to tell anybody. This is very private. I have problems. And yes, I have been seeing somebody. What happened was, it made me go within...within...within. And when I got as far "in" as I could go, I found out what was there. *(Pause.)*

Nothing! Absolutely nothing! So I can take on any role and make it my own because I have absolutely nothing to work with! When I am rehearsing a role, I light incense, I mumble, - - no - - I hummm - - no - - I CHANT. No! I cannot tell you what my chant is, it's very private. And I turn around in circles really fast. *(She does.)* It opens doorways. Well, it does. I don't care what you think. It does, and my doorways have been opened. Alright? oooohhh, to chant, to turn around in circles, and to act, that's living!!

A 1930'S MOMENT

AUTHOR'S NOTE: Staying up late one night during graduate school, I was watching some scratchy old black and white drama on TV. Taken with the transparency of the acting and directing and how **over the top** it was, I decided to turn off the sound and write new dialogue, taking all my cues from the characters' actions alone. It was great fun. The result is a highly unusual monologue for a very creative actress who is not afraid to take on a challenge. Use a British dialect of your choosing and play the humor. Attack your consonants, and have fun!

(There is also a male version of this monologue in this collection entitled "Another 1930's Moment.")

An actress auditions for a director of a black and white - - highly dramatic moment - - in an old 1930s film; clipped accent, nondescript. She watches the screen in front of her as she tries to figure out what the voice over would be, making it up as she goes along.

The window was blowing open and closed, open and closed. I lay there on the bed...dead. Yes, I believe I was quite dead. No! No, not quite dead. I move. I'm alive! Thank God, I'm alive. No. No, I'm still now. It is clear to me now more than ever that I am, quite and unshakably, dead. But I move! Still, I breathe and I move, now creeping towards the open window. I see him. I see him in all his un-fa-thom-able beauty. You must know what I mean. I stand here by the open window, and I look down at all his beautiful nakedness. I gasp and wish that I too was naked. But alas, I am not. Do I dare to disrobe here by the open fire - - I mean open window? Here. Here I too will disrobe and put on my delicate, sheer cotton dress.

And now, unlike no other moment, I walk along the steps on the cliff...looking attractive. He sees me now. Clothed, unlike before, he approaches me. He walks in front of me. Stop it! I don't like that. Walk alongside me or not at all... There. That's better. So much, so much - - Aah! Something has me, has me tightly in its grip, it's sin-ew-y, ugly dark grip. I look and to my horror I see it is his hands around my upper arm. "Let go!" I cry..."let go!" He lets go and shoots me a dark and dangerous stare like he wants to own me...drain me somehow.

Just then! The vicar arrives. Not a moment too soon. Oh, no...not a moment too soon. *(Breaks character now, completely different voice and attitude - - nasal, whiny voice.)* Is that alright, Mr. DeMille?

BEING ORDINARY

A frustrated young woman in her twenties explores what being ordinary means.

I was always afraid of not being somebody. Petrified of being ordinary. I tried being a secretary, but all I could think of was...a "suck-a -tery." Not the job for me. When the bosses would come in and ask me to do something for them, I'd always want to say to them, "Do it yourself! What am I? Your slave?" The thought of being a career secretary scared me to death. When I look at ordinary moms with their ordinary babies, it scares me. No way am I going to be just another mom or whatever. I want to do something with my life, really do something. All my brothers and sisters are boring, doing exactly what's expected of them. Forget it! I don't think any of my friends think like I do. They don't really care anyway. That's why I moved to New York City. There's such life here. Such possibilities. Around every corner, right? Well, all I've gotten is a two-bit apartment subleased to me by some cross-dressers, no friends, a horrible cough, rain and rude people. There's actually a guy down the hall from me who sings opera in the middle of the night. I can hear his roommate crying out "Shut-up! Shuuuuttttt-uuupppp!!"

It's creepy.

I'm beginning to wonder if being ordinary is not really all that bad. What do you think?

MY BROOM

A concerned wife discusses the changes in her husband's behavior, especially with her domestic tool, her broom.

Honey, can I talk to you? I have noticed some little changes in you of late that I would like to discuss with you - - openly. Take the broom - - for example - - it's always gone. You are always mumbling little incantations, chants, under your breath at the dinner table while passing the salt or while reading the paper. I have noticed that you like the color black - - a lot. What about the books from the library? Like this one here - - *Black Magic is Not All Black*? It does seem to me that if you are having a mid-life crisis, we should be able to talk about it together. Give me your hands, see there, your nails are getting a bit long - - you scratched me! Ow.

Hon, I have an interest in everything you do, you're my husband and I love you. But! The broom is always gone. You know it is not healthy to be flying around in all kinds of weather, not with your allergies. A plane could hit you. A flock of winged creatures could poop on you. I hate to complain. It's just that it's come to my attention that your diet is odd also. Read odd. You hardly eat, and when you do, well, God knows what you are brewing, eh, cooking! The smell is enough to kill a person. Or is that the point? I don't have problem with witches. Remember Samantha? Loved her! Honey, stop that mumbling, are you listening to me? Where are you going? Leave that here! Get your own!! Well, if you are a so-called *you-know-what* now, I wish at least you would go and buy your own damn broom!

CAREFUL

At their favorite restaurant, a woman in her thirties tries to hold on to a dying affair and scolds herself for not being careful enough.

Look, if we're real careful nobody has to ever find out. You have to be real careful about your looks. You know exactly what I'm talking about. There! There it is. If you could just stop feeling so guilty all the time. It's written all over your face. And you don't have to tell your wife everything. Sometimes...you can still love someone but not have to share all aspects of your life! You might want to keep quiet. Don't get that hurt look on your face. Come on. We have to get on with it. I know you still love Nicole. You've reminded me enough times. I'm married, too. You don't see me running to my husband to tell him everything. Look - - what are we doing here, playing house? Playing lovers? Look at me, Fabian. Put your beer down and answer me. We've had good times. Remember the woods? Your cell phone just kept ringing and ringing? Remember? What's wrong?

Oh, God...Nicole knows, doesn't she? You told her! My God, how could you be so stupid! This involves me too, you know. What did you say to her? Does she know it's me? Please tell me she doesn't. Well, that's great. I'm suppose to work with her next week on the church yard sale. I can just see it now. "How much should we charge for this, Nicole?" as she takes a knife out of her purse and stabs me. And we were so careful. I should have known not to get involved with a man who actually loves his damn wife. I wasn't careful enough. Next time, no more married men.

CHURCH

AUTHOR'S NOTE:
Having been brought up a good Catholic girl, I did indeed feel guilty for
years for not going to church. As the character in "Church" states, there are
many reasons for attending church. If it is out of love for one's parents, then
that should be as good a reason to attend a church as any. In this monologue,
the pain of the dying parents combined with the fear of being rejected and a
deep need for love on all levels is the challenge for the actor to capture.

*A woman confides in a priest about her newfound love of returning to the Catholic
church, as it now brings her the peace, love and closeness to God she has been
searching for.*

So you see, Father, seeing all those tubes going in and out, that hospital smell. I,
well, that is my parents are...well, not doing well...at all, and I looked around
for anything to help me feel close to them. I wanted to remember. Everything.
How it felt to be a little girl sitting between my parents. My dad with his
aftershave on - - how pretty my mom looked with one of her flowery hats on
and me wearing my shiny white shoes and petticoat. That petticoat was very
itchy. My mom says she almost had a heart attack when she turned around and
I had taken it off in church right before communion! Of course, I was three
years-old at the time, but I still hate petticoats, or slips as we call them today.

I know you'll understand. I just hope you won't judge me too harshly. But the
cathedral drew me in after twenty years of absence like an old lost friend. It was
the choir singing. I've always been a sucker for *Ave Maria*. I had to bite my lip
not to cry. I was kind of unbelievable that I was feeling what I was feeling. The
trinity makes sense to me now. It's like the connective tissue. You know?
Connecting **me** in - - somehow.

No more just going through the motions and saying the words without feeling. I'm glad I left because now I can really feel the mystery we call God. My mother and my father sit next to me. I sit next to them. I came back to the church out of love for them, and in return, I found what I've been searching for all these years. My path to love. Before it was too late.

Please, can I stay?

THE CLINIC

AUTHOR'S NOTE:
When I was in graduate school, I had to go to the university clinic and there was a very nervous young female student there, flipping through magazines. I couldn't hear what she was saying, but she did look very nervous. So I let her talk!

A nervous young college woman awaits her turn at a clinic, flips through a magazine and talks to a friend.

I hope they don't call my name. Oh! I thought they called my name. Is it scary in there? I mean, do they ask you a lot of personal questions? I can't calm down. I really do think I've got something. When I was growing up, I never remember thinking that boys could make you sick. They were suppose to make you feel good. Was I brain dead or what? I really didn't like it all that much either. I was so scared the whole time that my dorky roommate would show up. I do feel sorry for her though, having only one lung and all. *(Stands up.)*

What? Was that me? God, I wish they would just call my name and get it over with. If I do have some horrible disease from that guy, can they kick me out of school or anything? Do my professors have to know? I always thought that I was a nice girl, and now I'm sitting here waiting to be examined like a specimen. Can you come in with me? I know it's gross to ask, but I'm...

Oh, never mind. You do the crime, you do the time, right? What does a person do? You can't just stop and say, "I hate to ask you this, but do you happen to have your health file with you? Or your social security number handy so I could just plop you into my dating program and make sure you're not infected?" Life isn't very romantic anymore, is it? I'm only 19 years old, and I feel like I've lived the life of a harlot or something. Please tell me there's more to all this. Oh! This is it. Please come with me. Please?

THE CONFESSION

AUTHOR'S NOTE:
Being brought up Catholic, I spent a lot of time wondering about the sanctity of the confessional booth. One time I did go in and tell the priest that I had not sinned and wanted some extra blessings, and he laughed and laughed. Everything stays with a writer for a long time. I enjoyed getting to know Jezebel. This character is very colorful!

A young woman goes to a confessional, but she doesn't feel she has any sins to confess. Priest patiently listens.

Bless Me Father, for I have...not sinned. I just came in to get some extra blessings. That's okay, isn't it? I mean, I might have sinned, but I actually don't believe in the word sin. Oh! I hope I'm not offending you, you being a priest and all. It's just that it's so negative. YOU'RE A SINNER! *(Laughs.)* In today's society, if you don't mind me saying so, it just doesn't work. You see, these days, everybody is equal. Men and women, black and white, sinners and saints. So you see, I couldn't really come in here and honestly say I've sinned. That's like admitting I'm an outcast. And I am not an outcast.

Are you in there? Oh, good. Well, how about those blessings? Should I bow my head or something? I was sort of thinking that you could say some extra prayers for me using my name. Say my name out loud, then say an extra powerful prayer just for me. That way I'll get double, hey, maybe even triple the blessings! I have to go. It looks like there are some real sinners out here just dying to get in. Thanks for your time. Remember, say my name first. Oh! I forgot to tell you my name. It's Jezebel. Thanks!

DEAD MAN

A bitter woman visits the grave of her estranged husband in West Virginia.

A graveyard. It suits you. Poor, poor excuse for a human being. How could you have done that to me? Was I not suppose to care about my own mother? Was that my big mistake?

I died years ago! Now it's your turn, you... You know, I never wanted to curse. I thought it was the devil's language. But when you're playing with the devil himself, then you use his words. YOU BASTARD!!

You done me wrong, Charlie. You done me sooo wrong. I can't even visit Lewisburg without everyone whispering behind my back. "She's the one who ran off and deserted her poor family! Poor Charlie!" You must have just soaked up all that attention. All the women in town baking you pies. Are you listening, Charlie?

Do you know where you are, Buddy-boy? I'll tell you. You're buried six feet under, right next to the woman who had *abandoned* you when you were a child. Mother and child reunited at last! *(Laughs sarcastically.)* Wouldn't you just die? *(Throws dirt on grave.)* Too late.

DID COMMUNION WRONG

A visitor to a new church explains why she won't be coming back.

Well, I did communion wrong. There I said it. I don't know what happened. I was just walking up, like everyone else. When I got to the altar, there were two lines. I took the line on the left. As I got to the end of the line, an older man comes around the corner and gives me a really horrible look like, "if you don't move out of my way, you'll be sorry!" I just froze, I was so scared I had gone up the wrong way. I finally offered to move over, but he just kept staring at me like I was a heathen.

This was suppose to be a loving, holy moment of taking the host and believing you are ingesting the body of Christ. But instead, I felt like an unwilling host who was being eaten. Then it happened again! Another older gentleman comes around the corner and the same thing played out. This time, the lady behind me gave him her arm to hold onto. So, ashamed and wicked, I finally got to kneel down, and as I looked up at the priest, I could see the disappointment in his eyes.

Communion was ruined! What, is there a rule book for communion-etiquette somewhere? If there is, I need to get ahold of it. Oh, just wait, it gets worse. As I was getting through swallowing a large, bone-dry piece of host, I found myself walking down the center aisle of church to return to my seat. Again, the disapproving looks! I am damned to eternal hell for this, I just know it.

So, to answer your question. NO, I don't think I'll be coming back to your church anytime soon.

THE DREAM

A first time would-be mother shares a frightening dream with her best friend.

Well, it finally happened. This little baby, whatever it is, whoever it is, is supposed to arrive the 10th of July. So here I am as big as a house, none of my clothes fit me, and I'm taking on this eerie otherworldly feeling. My body's not my own anymore, as if it ever was. I am starting to feel the universal urge, the tug of the life force upon itself to recreate itself through me! It's not a thought, it's a reality. Hang in there with me, just let me ramble.

I thought motherhood was going to be so glamorous...I'd lie around the house looking maternal, very Madonna-like. It's as if I'm the only one who's ever been with child before.

There is this dream I keep having, over and over...

I'm in the desert, somewhere very far away, and a long, long time ago. I'm giving birth to a king, everyone is waiting outside the tent. All the colors are a golden muted yellowish hue as if I have tapped into someone else's life and my own all at the same time. I'm this exotic, dark-haired, very beautiful woman. There's a lot of pain. I know I'm going to die, but the baby is very important to the people. I was just a slave or a concubine, just a vehicle for the baby. Somehow, I'm not sad about it. I knew I had to pass over, I wasn't the important one.

Then I wake up. Am I going to die giving birth to this baby?

It's only a dream...I guess.

HOTEL STAY

AUTHOR'S NOTE:
When I had to arrange for two casting directors for Los Angeles to come to my small town to help teach a film acting intensive workshop, they brought L.A. with them. They complained about everything, and even though I put them up in a very nice, beautiful hotel, I was imagining what they were saying behind closed doors in their hotel room. Have fun with this one! And make sure you can visualize where everything is in the room.

A businesswoman yelling to her roommate in the bathroom in an expensive hotel that is not up to her standards.

Fran, would you look at the decor in here? What is this, early garage-sale? First they give us a smoking room. We change that. Okay. Now they give two grown women a room with one queen size bed and one hide-a-bed? Are they joking? Oh my God, I think I just saw a roach. Am I in a nightmare? Hey, did they give us any extra blankets or sheets? And where the hell are the pillow mints? I'm getting upset. Fran! Do you hear me? This place is $130 a night, and it's a dump. Did you smell that elevator? I thought for sure someone had died in there. Get out of the bathroom! If I don't strip butt naked and scrub this vomit smell off my body, I'm going to jump out this window.

What is this?? They have nailed the windows shut. Is this maximum security or what? *(Yelling.)* I can not take much more of this!! Oh thank God, they have a little bar. *(Tries it, won't open.)* Open! Open, damn you!! I need a drink, and I need one now. Fran, what are you doing in there? Oh my God, you have to put $5 worth of quarters into this stupid little bar to get a drink. How about I just pick it up and throw it through the window? That'll solve both problems. I'm having a heart attack out here. Hurry up!! Fran? Fran...you alright in there? *(Looks around.)*

I want my teddy...

I'M EXCITED

A woman tries to deal with the fact that she's not been chosen to continue in her job after major budget cuts.

Budget cuts. Only two but very cruel words. Of course, I'm excited about where I'll be going. I just wish I knew *where* I was going. Well, I'm sorry, too. I'll try and hold my head up high as I stagger through my last long walk past the leaking water fountain, the whiny accountant and the smell of the rotting leftover lunches in the employee lounge. I'll even try and pretend that no one is talking about me and silently thanking God they weren't fired.

Hey! Do you think I came off as too enthusiastic, is that why the bigwigs didn't want me around? Do you think they thought I wanted their jobs? Do you want my "I'm better than anyone else" sign? Yeah, you're right, I'll trash it. What about my little zen garden? It never really helped anyway.

No one can say I didn't give my all. I really cared about the business. I knew all the little secrets around here, also. OH! Do you think I knew TOO much? It's like that old Hitchcock, I think it was Hitchcock, black and white movie, "The Man Who Knew Too Much," except I'm a woman. I often felt they wanted to push me down "the thirteen steps." It does give me "high anxiety." Okay, enough with the movie metaphors. Well, that's everything. I wish I could pack myself into one of those containers. One that doesn't hurt as much. But hey! Must be positive, glass half-full and "all that jazz." They say it's lonely at the top. It's also devastating at the bottom. But I'm excited, nonetheless... I really am...excited I'm going to a great new world. Somewhere...over the...

I'M SORRY

A woman tries to explain her lack of feeling for a lover before her family returns.

I'm sorry. I really am. It was never supposed to go this far. You knew my circumstances. I can not abandon everything I know for a whim. I'm sorry. But that's all you've been to me. A whim. Don't you think I know that's a cruel word? What are you doing? What are you doing with that? Put that down, you can't have that. No, WE didn't buy that together. That is mine. It is too, my grandmother gave it to me. You know that - - give it to me!! *(He drops it, she reacts to the broken piece of her heritage.)*

My God, you broke it. That was my Grandma's. I dreamt about this! I was there…crouching over a dead deer, in the mist, in the woods, lost and unable to decide which way to turn or what to do. I was so scared and confused. Another big male deer walked towards me - - like it was accusing me - - took my breath away. I remember I turned and saw…you, I was mouthing something. What was I saying? What was it??

Oh! God, they're here. Please, now I'm begging you. Just take anything you want, but just leave. What?? What do you want me to do? To say it, you need to hear it? Okay, it's true. Yes, yes, it's true. I don't feel anything for you, nothing at all. Please leave now!!

Wait! Now, I remember. I remember what I was saying to you in the forest. I was saying, "Help me, help me, help me to decide"!

Ah, the doorbell, they're here. There's no time for this, there's never enough time. Go.

THE LEAD

An actress shares her disappointment and frustration with a rival actress with a friend.

Oh, I got the lead alright. Bittersweet as it was. Everything in my life was just grand. Then she showed up. You know who I'm talking about. I don't want to say her name. But we were both at the audition, and I made it perfectly clear to her the role was MINE and MINE alone. Do you know what she did? The tramp. She excused herself from the readings and left! Don't you see what she's done to me? She's put me into a prison.

I walk out onto the stage for my opening monologue. I look out into the audience and there she is! - - staring at me. Daring me to be good. Daring me to take the stage while she sits and stares. And watches me. I could feel my energy being drained by her. Like a vampire. I think she should be banned from all professional theatres.

She won. That's the whole point. Don't you see? She's sitting out there knowing that I didn't win the role on my own. She *gave* it to me. How can I enjoy acting when I know my rival's out there gloating? It's not fair. How could this happen to me? I'll tell you one thing. I WILL NEVER AUDITION FOR ANOTHER PLAY AGAIN!

I'll beat her at her own game.

LIZANNE ON THE PHONE

A young housewife is on the phone trying to get a new friend to let her babysit her children.

Well, why don't you just let me babysit little Joey and Melissa? I'm sure they'll be fine. You work so hard and deserve to have a night out with your husband. You're always complaining that your kids drive you crazy and that you'd do anything to get away. Well, here's your chance. I will be happy to either come over and watch them or you can bring them here. What? What do you mean I wouldn't know what to do? What exactly does that mean? Have you forgotten that I already have two children of my own? Sarah is still only a baby. All babies cry! That's what they do, for God's sake. They aren't going to just lie there all day.

If you don't mind me saying so, it's a little insulting to me that you don't trust me with your baby and little girl. And while we're on the subject, I think you tend to scream an awful lot. And oh yeah, what was that bruise on little Joey's arm the other day? The big scratch on Melissa's face? Huh? Huh? If I were you, I'd take a good look in the mirror. If there is an ax-murderer loose, it's you, honey. I thought we were buds. You've seen too many "Lifetime for Women" movies. If I was a wacko, I'd have killed off my kids a long time ago. I'm kidding! It's a joke.

Now, are you still my best friend…or not?

LOOK AT HER

AUTHOR'S NOTE:
After watching a Barbara Walters' interview with Princess Diana, I wrote this monologue. Make sure you place the invisible video camera that is taping you in front of you with the invisible television DL or DR of you. Feel the palpable fear of this young cook...

Frightened young female cook for the royal family looks at tape of Princess Diana in her last interview with Barbara Walters as her boyfriend tapes her own interview at the same time.

She's scared. Look at her. Look at the way she twitches and looks down. What really gives it away are her eyes. Like a mouse cornered. I know because I feel the exact same way. No, keep that tape of her going and now tape me at the same time. **Do it!** Ready?

T takes deep breath.

I'm just a cook in the kitchen. I'm nobody really...but my ears, my ears betray me...my peace - - I overheard, don't you understand? I overheard everything. She was **MURDERED**, for God's sake! Every detail laid out like a giant puzzle. That's why I'm taping myself with her together so you'll know if anything happens to me, well, you'll just know it was the same people. The people - -

(Whispers.) In the Royal Game of Chess, the Queen takes all.
Later—or sooner than later, the pawn will also fall. *(Pause.)*

She's scared. Look at her.

MICHELLE'S TIRADE

A wife laments her husband's long absences.

I don't know where your stupid clubs are. It's a golf club, not a person, a piece of wood, dead wood!! Take it easy, you'll find it. Well, while you're gone, I suppose you should know that I'll probably be in a special hospital on the lowest level of heaven where it will take me years to repair my soul to recuperate. Why? Because of doing away with myself. They'll make me see movies of all the pain I've caused. Why, you say, honey? Why is that? Well, dear, because you are never home, you are always off to Bangkok, Saudi Arabia, or even to Montana, for Christ's sake. Doing what? Why...not saving the world, but golfing!! That's right, you'd rather be out golfing somewhere than at home with your loving wife. I can't be around knives anymore. I, Michelle, your wife, am now considered one of the five "d's" - - Dangerous. I also might add "in distress" to that list. Of course, you'll hardly skip a beat. "Oh, my wife's dead. Hmmm... I wonder if I should play the "back 9" or the "front 9" this tournament, or maybe both since I don't have to rush home?"

I HATE YOU, I HATE YOU, I HATE YOU, DO YOU HEAR ME?

Phone rings.

Oh, hi, Boo, no, nothing, just doing my things. Oh, that's alright, you take as long as you like. I'm fine.

MY MOTHER'S HANDS

AUTHOR'S NOTE:
This piece is adapted, using artistic license, from an original short story written by Julya Oberg, whom I met while in graduate school in Virginia. Her story was so moving that I wanted to give the daughter a stronger voice to be heard, even as her mother is dying. This is a dynamic, dramatic original piece that could work very well for an audition piece. You can make a lot of strong acting choices and show your prowess as an actress. Work the beats!

A young woman in her twenties talks to her mother as she lies dying in a hospital room.

(To nurse as she leaves.) She's in here? Can I have a moment? Thank you. Here you are. I don't know. I don't know how I feel. That's the worst of it, Mother. You're my mother, always have been and always will be. Why didn't you love me? Huh? All those years, all those times of ignoring me, forgetting to pick me up at school, not taking me to birthday parties, coming home late and leaving me alone, and then standing there, just looking at me...watching me sleep. I've got news for you. You thought I was asleep, but I never was. Just like you might be doing to me now. Escaping your motherhood duties to me one final time. The difference between us, Mother, you see, is that I can't escape being your daughter. There's no escape hatch. No, "this way out." I can't escape...loving **you.** No matter how many angry faces you gave me.

I want to get married, I want to have children, but it's not in the cards. The cards you dealt. Even my body hates me, too. You should know I have cancer. Cervical. Never even had the chance to use it...

(Trying not to cry, picks up her mother's hands.) They're so dry!

(Puts lotion on her mother's hands.) There, there, that's better. Funny, isn't it? You should be comforting me. Of course, it's your hands that tie us together forever. Our hands are exactly alike. I look down at my hands and see yours. They are pretty…delicate, aren't they?

Please, Mother, tell me that you loved me, even if it's a lie. Please, I don't care. I just want to hear it. Blink, blink for me, anything! Tell me to be brave, tell me it's not my time, tell me I'll get over this. Tell me it's going to be alright.

(To nurse.) Okay, they're ready for me? No matter what happens in my surgery down the hall, we'll always have our hands.

OLD AGE

AUTHOR'S NOTE:
When I visited my father in his nursing home and I turned around and saw the look on my mother's face and how her whole body seemed to be caving in from the guilt and helplessness of her own situation, these thoughts started to run through my head. In fact, in later life, a lot of the masks we hold up can no longer be held, and we say and do things to each other that end up hurting the feelings of the younger generation. Play this monologue for real.

Middle-aged woman expresses her disappointment in her elderly parents to her husband.

I'm petrified of growing old. Dad's seventy-five years old, and he's dying. He's demanding and mean. He screams about his stupid coffee not being the right temperature. I could see the heartbreak when Mom put him into that nursing home. Those ghostly old people, the hopelessness! Guilt descended around her like a heavy black cloud. She didn't say anything, but I'm sure she was reliving the pain when she had to put her own mother into a nursing home. Grandma. I think the stress is getting to Mom. She's become very sharp-tongued in her old age. She'll just tell you exactly what she thinks of you now. I went to visit her, and we were sitting there having tea, and she starts in on me about how she's always hated my clothes. I almost dropped my cup. I'm thinking, what is she talking about? My clothes? Does that mean that she's never really accepted me for who I am? Ever? Or was that not my mom talking?

The horror is that I'm probably going to have to put her in a home soon. How am I going to handle this? I want my mother back. I don't want her to be mean and to say nasty things to me. I don't want her to be old anymore. I want to look at her face and feel like I'm home. You're going to have to help me. I'm connected to her so that means that when she goes, I go. Is that what that means?

I find myself looking at her and wanting to scream, "Where's my mother? What have you done with her?" God help me and her.

QUEEN OF ACADEMICS

Frustrated teacher wears a cheap tiara, rants in faculty lounge.

What are you staring at? Because I feel like it, alright? If you don't like it you can just go get your own 79 cent cheap plastic pink tiara with feathers, and you can be queen of the day, too. I am worth it, and I'm wearing it. Yes! - - for the rest of the day! No, I will not move over or share my watermelon pickles.

(Points to her tiara.) You are in the presence of royalty. No more wimpy whiny people who gossip about anything that moves. I can't stand them. I want them all beheaded, even if it was outlawed years ago.

I wish I could take my head off, just for a while. For a rest. Just lay it there next to my coffee cup and computer and my "while you were out" phone messages that I never return. I loathe those little pink memos. I hereby declare there to be no more pink memos or any memos of any kind! And while I'm making declarations, no more deadlines, no more committee meetings, no more assessments, no more decisions, no more thoughts, no more eating, no more - - wait!! Back up, back up, no more eating? What the hay?? I might be rambling. It's my tiara, it's crooked. Okay, so my head can stay.

I'm just having a real bad day, okay? So let me sit here and drink my diet Orange Fanta and be a queen for the day, or…just for a moment, a tiny regal moment. Then I'll calm down and only send a couple of colleagues to the dungeon. Ahh, the joy of that thought. *(Takes off tiara.)*

That's better. All done. Pickle?

ROSES

An inexperienced teenage girl shares her tale of an unusual date with her friend.

So he invites me over to his house - - he got rid of his parents for the night. He has Italian chicken in the oven, a doily tablecloth on the table, very "Leave-it-to-Beaver." Anyway, after we eat and talk, he takes me up to his bedroom, and guess what is all over his bed? Go ahead, guess. You'll never guess in a million years. **Rose petals!!**

Helloo!

Okay, so I'm standing there thinking, "Gee, I wonder what he has in mind?" I mean, come on, I just met the guy. I thought, "hey! a free dinner, watch a movie, but Alan - - that's A-L-A-N, with one "L," that's his name, has ideas of his own. What did he think I was? Some bimbo or something?

Well, as the evening wore on, I calmed down a bit. Watched a movie. Talked some more. He's a gentle person, kinda sweet. Nobody has ever cared what I think or feel. Alan *listened*, with these incredible blue eyes that you could get lost in. Turns out he didn't want to do anything, you know, just loved the movie, "American Beauty" with all those rose petals. He's a real movie buff. It was the movie. He wanted to do something special, just for me.

Daisies used to be my favorite. Now roses are...

SEE ME?

Mixed up your girl tries to connect with others to feel alive.

Hi. I didn't see you out there. You startled me. You shouldn't sneak up on people like that. It's rude. See my pink dress? I'm a movie star. Yes, I am. Up here, *(Points to her head.)* I am. I could be, anyway. Maybe not a grand star, but something...shiny, catches your eye. Like in the night sky, all twinkly up there. I'd like for everyone to be looking at me, twinkling. That's a fun word, isn't it? Do you have a fun word? Everyone should have at least one. Everyone look up and see me! See my great big...swirling mess? Thousands of things mixed...I'm lost in there...and here...somewhere...I'm in here somewhere.

It's good to be something important. I haven't made it yet. But I will. If you would look at me like I'm important, it would help. Look at me like you see me, hear me? I'm tired of looking up all the time. I'm the only voice, wearing the only dress. Behind a wall of invisible atoms. I could reach out for a helping - - hear the music? That's the planets singing, like Aristotle said. I surprised you, didn't I? How could a simple thing know about singing planets? I'm spinning and I'm singing, but no know sees me. If they did, then that must be what heaven is like. No more mess.

SOMETHING'S COMING

AUTHOR'S NOTE:
For a long time, I realized that I carried around the thought that I was special somehow...different. But then I talked to some friends of mine, and several of them had the same thought. So this monologue was a way to hear this universal song and desire to belong to worlds we can not even comprehend.

Male or female has had a surreal experience and tries to makes sense of it to best friend.

Do you feel that? That! It's like I'm being recognized by a higher court, a higher level of being-ness, and am being invited to join them. There's steps, I can sense them, and I'm being shown the stairs, the steps of Saturn or somewhere similar. It's a much, much greater universe. I'm being singled out. I know something wonderful is coming to me. I feel it. It's like the veil is being lifted for me and I am in touch with what all the great artists have been silent witnesses to - -

I'm not just a body. I knew it all along. We are all part of something so much bigger, so much grander. All the hard work and intense focus on my writing has somehow sent a message out to the cosmos. I wonder if I'm sending out a certain color or vibration? I think I might meet Einstein and Lincoln and all the other great spirits. But I can sense that they are not those people anymore, sort of meshed into a larger picture. Wow...

Do you think I might be revealing a sacred event? Do you think I could make all this attention to myself go away by angering the great ones somehow? I don't think so. The energy is too positive and different. Something great is coming my way. I just have to be patient. Meanwhile, I'll continue to collect stars in my bucket.

THE QUAGMIRE

Young woman at new job feels the brunt of gossip and backstabbing, practices what she'll say to boss.

Why is it like this? I don't want to turn into something I don't want to become. The innuendos, the lies, the words flying behind closed doors. Are the looks what they seem? Are they…WHAT are they? Please, make sure I don't become like those awful people. Jake, do you think I'm overreacting? First, there is the smile, then the frown, then the outright rejection, then the - - I mean. I don't know who I can trust - - is what I'm feeling so unreal that I must talk about them like this to you, force them out like a dirge in a scene? I know I'm dramatic, everyone reminds all the time. Friends that I thought - - ah! - - how I thought. Jake? I guess I didn't think at all. So what if I'm dramatic, it's who I am, dammit!

Hands reaching out to me from the depths, from the quagmire. I can't shake it off. Do I stay within this swamp or rise above it? What if it's the same elsewhere? Jake, what's if it's me? Am I a bad person?

What have I said - - or done - - what? What did I do? What? I'm not used to people not liking me. I am the quagmire. I'm ashamed. I have, at some time, done everything I now hate being done to me. If I go to another job, it will just start over, right, Jake? I would like to rest from all this. I don't really like people at all.

(Pause.) Well, I can't say any of this to him; he's probably at the forefront of all of this.

My stomach hurts.

WISHING WELL

A melancholy yet hopeful woman wishes for her ultimate good at a wishing well in a large city park.

I don't even know if you are a wishing well. You're more of a wishing pond, and a man-made one at that. Please don't be offended.

(Digs for a coin.) Give me a minute, I know I have a penny in here somewhere. Ahh, a penny. I wish more than anything in the world, well, you know what that is. Dear well, how do I know what I am if I'm alone? There's no one to bounce things off of or to smooth out the edges or to define where the edges are.

(Digs for another penny.) Oh, and I also hereby wish and proclaim to the entire universe that I want my job to work out here, if it is for the highest good of all manking. Manking? Who's writing this stuff? Oh, yeah, I am. I'm suppose to be a writer. Bear with me, I have a couple of more wishes.

(She throws another coin in.) Please let my mother stay healthy and have a safe journey to my sister's. You know she's been through enough, two heart operations, and that is a long trip. Please watch after her.

(Throws in a couple of more coins.) Oh, hell, here's some more, just please, honestly, make this work, all of it.

(Starts to walk away, then turns back and dumps her entire change purse in the pond.) Here! What do you want from me? Blood? Take it all. Take everything. Since I'm a prisoner of my own thoughts, and I have to go through this trial of social isolation, take it all! You and I have to become good friends. We have something in common anyway. The silence. I wish I could learn to be more calm like you. What the hell, I'd jump in myself if I thought it would help. Seriously, please, make my wishes come true. Remember Mickey, *(She sings softly.)* "When you wish upon a star…makes no difference who you are…"

(Starts to walk away slowly, then turns.) Oh, by the way, keep the change.

PART TWO:
MALE MONOLOGUES

ANOTHER 1930'S MOMENT

An actor takes to the microphone (voice-over) following the action and filling in the secret thoughts of the character on the screen; clipped, non-descript accent; a very slow and dramatic moment of a bit of a 1930's romantic drama, auditioning for the director.

I can remember the air that morning, crisp and free. Free-doom that I had never felt before. Where, I say again, where did this feeling come from? Why, I remember. I remember as if it was just yesterday... In fact, it was yesterday. I looked down and saw. To my amazement, I saw that I was naked. Born free. Indeed. My tanned, muscled, oiled, slick, rather handsome bare flesh, free. I feel like I could fly! Like Ithacus. Ithcus... Whatever. There in the window, I see her. She's staring and staring and staring... **What** are you staring at? I realize we are both staring. But she has her clothes on. I can't let that get me down. I can't allow my brain cells to go a place they shouldn't go. Bad cells.

I throw on my light cotton pants, barely zipped, and rush up to greet her. She greets me rather rudely. She says...something. I don't know.

(To director - - actor's real voice.) I wasn't listening. I have a problem with listening.

(Acting again.) So I start to sing a little ditty about our special singing pool. I laugh now to think of her laughing eyes. Why is the whole world laughing? I need to grab her and let her know that I don't like that. "Stop it! Stop it, I say!" I am just about to lose my patience with her, when just then, the nosy vicar arrives. That teeny tiny vicar from Gulliver's Travels wearing that stupid little black dress and sandals. Be a man!! Change your clothes and wear pants, like me. Little cotton pants that zip properly.

But I back down now and take a deep breath. She's stepping on my toes and the vicar is doing something unmentionable on my pants.

(Actor's whiny nasal voice.) Eh! Mr. DeMille, like, uh, is that alright? 'Cause if it's not, I can do it again. I'm really beginnin' to feel the guts of this character, ya know?

BLACKBEARD IN THERAPY

AUTHOR'S NOTE:
I wrote this monologue as a prospective piece for a new radio show being aired in Virginia. At the time, I was taking my fourth psychology course as part of my Drama Therapy foundation coursework. It seemed a natural humorous situation to put a pirate with an identity crisis in a psychologist's office to explore his "issues." The piece is almost 4-5 minutes long, but it could be cut anywhere to make it a one or two minute monologue. Could be a good curtain raiser if you were doing a variety show of some sort. Blackbeard is a lot of fun here.

Here the infamous BlackBeard is talking to his psychologist because he just hasn't been himself lately and feels a change)

Lie down here, then? *(Bounces on sofa.)* Comfy - - 'preciate it. Aye, aye, I knows I can talk about anything here and that yooou jist want the best for me, to help git me back into my own tale, so to speak - - but I haven't been myself lately, ye see. I'm not takin' to the killin' and pillagin' and lustful moonlit drinkin' bouts like I used to. It's just not fun anymore. I needs more. It's not workin for me to bees walkin' around with a large feathered entity on me shoulder anymore, mate. It's the constant cawking and clawing. It's interminable. Look, mate, I've got a boo-boo on my shoulder, here, right here, ah, where'd it go?? Eh... I guess it's the other shoulder, here. I gets confused from all the digging for treasure and ne'er havin my thirst quenched, but look ye here at it - - **DON'T TOUCH IT DON'T EVER TOUCH IT!**

Yo-ho! there, I'm sorry, I jist feels a bit odd these days, ya know - - not my real self. I think I'm having an identity crisis - - ya knows, "the individual versus the collectivism." I'm really an introvert in an extrovert society of murderers, thieves - - good people!

(Laughs pirate-like.) Eh... I've also been doin' a bit of readin', hangin' out at the local library - - that's not right, is it? Yes, yes, I need help! That's why I'm sitting here with ya, and **IF YOU DON'T LISTEN TO EVERY FRIGATE WORD I SPIT OUT, IT'LL BE THE PLANK FER YOU.** Yes, I'd love some tea. It will calm me down, yes, sweetner would be lovely. There's I go again! Did you **hear that?** I guess it jist gets old, well, trying to live up to my namesake - - it's a lot of pressure. I've changed, I don't even like beards. What? Word association - - okay, I'm greedy for anything.

I can start? Lovely - - **AGAIN WITH THAT WORD!!** See how these words don't ally with being a pirate - - just keep slipping out of me hole? OK, OK, I'll start. Sword, kill, kute, kitten, I love kittens. I was going to talk to you about that also. Cannons, bulls-eye, mayhem, death, skeletons, Halloween, candy, children, laughter, gaiety! *(Changes tone to be girl-like.)* Oh, it's no use, me heart yearns. I don't think I should be using words like yearn, do ye? Sorry, it must be me shoulder, it hurts so. Anyhoo, I picks up this pamphlet full of pirate histories I found next to the Aztec gold I've been hunting all these years on the high seas, and it gets me thinkin, what's the end of me tale? It never has gone well for any of us who stare the wind and sea spray down from coast to coast. What's my main joy, buccaneer? I've frittered away drink and food and the pleasures of the flesh until I don't feel alive anymore. The movie <u>Pirates of the Caribbean</u> really wreaked havoc on me mortality and now I feel like I've got a curse to be, well, non-pirate-like.

It's like this, I want to trade my parrot in for a kitten, white and fluffy preferably, one that I'd be callin' Powderpuff - - don't ye be smilin at me, for I'd just as soon put you into a stone chest that lies at the bottom of the sea - - well, not really - - and I'd like to start to take voice and diction classes to clean up me speech, and finally do a rewrite on this here pamphlet, and I'll call it "My Pirate, Myself." Let me tell ya how I feel - - I feel I needs your permission, like - - to abandon me men and to never return. To lay down me shooters, wash me hands of gunpowder and stale liquor and start over.

I want, I want, I want to shave my beard and pick out a new name and what? what? the old hour glass is empty already? So it 'tis...so it 'tis... I'll see you next time I be sailing around the bend...

Uh, could I take me tea with me?

BLUE FOOD

AUTHOR'S NOTE:

Flipping through a magazine in a waiting room, a photo of a blue teapot (in an article about food) and another photo of a large batch of pansies caught my eye. During the time, I was also having dealings with lawyers and the different worlds all came together in this quirky man's life. This monologue is included in a collection of *The Best Men's Stage Monologues of 1999*.

It has also been a very popular audition piece for actors.

Randy talks to a coworker at a company party about his wife's need to serve him feminine food.

What color is that? Ugh, no thank you. I don't like to eat blue food. There is something amiss in this world. I come home from a hard day's work, and my wife presents me with a cake that she made with a blue teapot on top of it and expects me to be excited. I work with murderers all day, and I can't deal with edible teapots when I get home. She meets me at the door with this silly grin on her face wearing an apron from the fifties and drags me into the kitchen to show me her latest creation. I'm under a doctor's care from her last attempt. Don't get me wrong. I love my wife. For her birthday, I got her a series of baking lessons from "Henri." "Henri" is a little frilly man. Come to think of it, ever since those classes, I have been fed a lot of pretty, feminine food. Mini-quiches, finger cucumber sandwiches? Huh? Huh?? And I can tell you right now, I don't like it. No, sir. Don't like it at all. Look here, is it wrong for me to want manly food? I wear manly clothes, I want manly food. What? Oh, I don't know. Steak, I guess. That really sounds macho, doesn't it? How about homemade lasagna? Things that remind me of my mother.

I miss Mother. She never fed me blue food. Mother wants to know why I had to choose such an unfriendly occupation, being a lawyer. Criminals are friendly. They are. I caught one bending over talking to a lone pansy sticking out of the concrete the other day. Just talking away. I didn't get too close. I wonder if he would eat a sugar teapot? Probably. My mother never would have dreamed of feeding her "big boy" blue food. Never. Just not manly enough.

CHEATING

AUTHOR'S NOTE:
This monologue comes from a time when I was an undergraduate theatre student in Texas and was accused of cheating in a Theatre History exam. Of course, I was not cheating, but I was called into the very scary professor's 9th floor office away from the theatre department and was scared to death by his threats to me. The feeling of being falsely accused of something, not even that heinous, is quite frightening. So this adolescent boy is speaking for all of us who have ever been accused of something they did not do.

A young cadet in a military high school accused of cheating pleads his case and for his life.

Sir, I know this looks bad. With all due respect, I'd like to plead my case. I was under a lot of pressure to get an "A" on this test. You see, I have a bad habit of writing down my notes on little pieces of paper, and I pulled them out so I could study them right before the test. I realize now how stupid that was. But please, believe me, I did not look at these notes during the test. I did not cheat.

Ever since I've been suspended, I've lost everything. I ask myself, what is this going to do to my family? I swear to you, and to God, and to all my classmates, that I did not cheat. Sir, my father and my grandfather have both graduated from Claiborne Military Academy. It is a family tradition that I would never jeopardize. I must graduate with my classmates. My family's honor is at stake. I have nowhere else to go. I could never face the disappointment on my father's face. If you find me guilty of cheating, you will end it all for me right here. My future is in your hands. Look at me for who I am.

I am innocent.

I SAID NO

A teenage boy in his first trouble with the law tries to get his mother to listen to how he feels.

That's why I don't want to go see a counselor! I don't want to talk to anyone. It won't do any good. Listen! Listen to me. I know myself, and I know that just sitting around talking won't do anything. Well, I'm not going. Why should I? No one cares how I feel. I mean, what are they going to ask me anyhow? Mom! No, no, you listen. You never listen to me. First of all, I didn't do anything. Abduction? Are they crazy? I'm sixteen years old, for Christ's sake. That girl had no business flipping us off. Why doesn't she go and talk to a stupid counselor? ARE YOU LISTENING TO ME? Mom, stop! You say I never talk to you and now I'm talking.

(Pause.) I don't know what I'm afraid of. The only way I can deal with this mess is by pushing it down and pretending that none of it happened. Look, I got kicked off the soccer team, my best friends have stabbed me in the back, and my girlfriend dropped me. Yeah, I'm doing real fine. I just don't feel like telling all of this to a perfect stranger.

(Pause.) Well, do you think it would help my case? Alright...I don't want to go to prison.

I'M HERE

AUTHOR'S NOTE:
I've been working with troubled adolescents, and the talk of being in trouble at school and having to go talk to the principal accompanied by young men who have grown up in the foster care environment sparked this monologue. No matter what they've been through, they desperately need and want someone to notice them as unique people. Say that last line right at the audience for a moving last moment.

Young man sits, waiting to talk to principal for leaving pictures of himself in a girl's locker. He talks to another student who is in trouble in the office.

I thought she'd like it, ya know, having an actual picture of me. Her locker was right next to mine and - - oh, excuse me - - ? Do you think he's going to get all loud and throw things at me? Well, I don't know, that's why I'm asking. Geez! Everyone's so sensitive around here. *(Turns to other student.)* Hope they don't put me in juvie. You don't want to go to juvie. I've already been there once, for six weeks, said I was incorrigible, whatever that means. The place smelled bad. I cried a lot. UH...did I just say that out loud, bro?

(Pause.) Cherie likes me. I know she does. Why did she have to go and blab to her mom that I'm supposedly stalking her all the time? That's harsh. Whatever. Man, have you seen the way she looks at me?

(Stands up.) Oh, oh, I thought he was motioning for me to go in - -

(He sits back down.) He looks alright. Authority isn't really my scene anyway.

What? Oh, I can't even remember. I think this is the third high school I've been to in three years. Man, a man, there's got to be something for me - - to connect with. I'm like a lego that's been left out after playtime is over. First family, now school - - geeeezzz. Even though the principal's probably gonna really let me have it, maybe he'll, at least, not hate me. I might even hit the jackpot, and he'll like me! That's a red-letter day.

(Other student goes into the principal's office.) Like an owl - - someone who will give a hoot. HHOOOooo….

I am here, aren't I?

IN THEM HILLS

A AAA man driving a tow-truck with a stranded lady's broken van towards a small town in the hills of West Virginia shares his reincarnation story with her while she sits there across from him, very uncomfortable.

I tell ya' one thing right now...there's gunna be 'nother civil war in this here country. Mark my words. Mark 'em. Sure as I'm sittin' here, there's a war brewing right now. I'm ready. Oh, yeah. In my basement is a whole truckload of weaponry. Been collectin' for years. Yep, me and my buddies are locked and loaded. Not goin' to be a racial thing, nope, this time - - it's taxes. When a fella can't even feed his kids, have health insurance for his family, it's a damn shame. An American disgrace. It's not right.

I know all about the Civil War, where all the battles around here took place. See that creek over yonder? There was a biggie there. Hundreds of Confederates died there. I have to say, even though I believed in their cause, I'm a true Yankee at heart. Two of my great-great uncles fought and died at Gettysburg. Ever been there? It's the smell you can't forget. The gut-wrenching fear. Boys and men alike, crying...

Not sure why I came back. Guess God got tired of me bein' a ghost. Wandering those old nasty scenes of death and decay... Looks like I might have to do the whole thing all over again. Never should have bayoneted that youngster. Death-grip means a whole different thing - - the way that boy held onto it and me as I was - - Those baby blue eyes. Those damn eyes. I look in the mirror. Guess what? I have the same baby blue eyes. What kind of joke is this?

Still have a scar where the bullets went into me. Had 'em at birth. Wanna see 'em? No need to get screamish on me.

(Pause.) The darndest part of it all is that the new civil war in our country probably won't even take place while I'm alive - - this time - - huh!. That just sucks. Ya know? A man can hardly feel he's worth anything if he don't fight about something.

I've done it once, I can do it again. Otherwise, no point in me being here. Well, what do you think? Hey! You weren't listening. **YOU WEREN'T EVEN LISTENING TO ME!!**

AAA or not AAA, I've got a good mind to drop you and your damn junk car off right here. But I'm not, because I'm an American. A true American wouldn't drop off a defenseless woman in the mountains of by-God West Virginia. Unless she asked for it...

LET ME FINISH

A gentleman faces everyone's worst fear, the slow humiliation of being moved to a smaller office. Here he confronts the boss' decision to move him

.

Excuse me. You asked to see me? If this is not a good time, I can come - - Oh, oh, okay. Sit here. Are you sure? Because the word out there is that anytime you ask someone to sit here, it's trouble. What did I do? Sorry, sorry to interrupt, to plunge ahead. Okay, okay, I'll be quiet now. Ssshh.

(Pause.) What?

(Pause.) Why? Why can't I just stay where I am? Not working hard enough? Who told you that? Whom? All I do is work. And those two slackers, excuse the deranged term, are never around themselves to know whether I'm slacking or not! You know, if you want to really know who is a slacker, much less a thief, I'll tell you. I'll just tell you. I've seen Tom himself steal coffee and sugar from the break room and bring it into his own office. Sheila collects sticky notes. You should just go into her desk and look. Me, I'm - -

Why do I have to move? This is just so unfair! If anyone should move it should be Sarah. Did you know, for example, that she made Angie cry when she told her she couldn't light her incense or listen to her wave machine? And Sarah told Agnes she couldn't bring her new baby to work ever. She makes everyone a nervous wreck. It's not right. Her office should be moved.

But I painted that office, those are my rugs, my curtains, my design. Come on, please, no, really, please, I've given my heart and soul to this job with very little pay, I don't ask for bonuses, even though God knows I deserve it, let me, let me, LET ME FINISH! DAMMNNNN'TTT LET ME TALK FOR ONCE!!

I can not be humiliated in front of the entire office by being moved to a smaller one. How am I suppose to hold my head up in a dingy little office? They're going to think I'm dingy. Lose respect for me. Please. NO, I mean, really...*please, please.*

I'll follow whatever new rules you want to give me, take shorter lunches, stop all gossip, submit my reports on time, but that office, my office, is my home away from home. I stay here late so I don't have to go home. There's nothing there. My office, it's all I've got. Don't make a grown man beg. It's all I've got. It's all I've got.

ROBERT'S MOUSE

A professional man comes screaming out of his office - - like a girl - - when a dead mouse falls off a shelf onto him.

AAAAhhhhh!!! Oh, oh, ohhh... AAaahhh!!! Oh my God! Oh my God!!! There's a - - there's a, I can't even say the word. A brown, creepy, a mouse! A dead mouse in there!! It fell on me. I'm not good at this... I was reaching for some paper, and it fell on me! This body has had a dead smelly mouse on it! Oh, oh, oh!!! I need a shower, I need something, something...

(Breathing heavily, trying to catch his breath.) We have a situation here. I can't go back in there. You have to understand something about me. I have two phobias. Heights and mice. Stairs or elevators, forget about it. My gutters haven't been cleaned out, well, ever. Ladders makes me tremble. Feel my hands! *(Shows sweaty palms to secretary.)* They are soaking wet. *(Mops brow.)* I'm breaking out in a cold sweat here.

Gotta get a grip. There's the mouse in there. Yes, we have a dead mouse in there. That's what we have. Ohhh, I have to sit down. No, not in there! How am I ever going to be able to go back into my office? I don't feel so well. Yes, that's a good idea, maybe I should go outside.

What? You'll take care of it? Oh, no, I couldn't make you do something like that. But thank you. No, no, no - - would you?

Wait. Just wait. Let me catch my breath. I'll be okay. Just give me a minute. *(Gaining control of himself.)* Now. We have to have a plan. A battle plan. The enemy is in there. We are out here. That sounds like a good plan. Okay, I've got it. If you'll go in there, I'll hand you the dustbin. I'll drop it on the floor. Then I'll run. No, no, I'll face up to this. This is something I have to face up to. You push the, you know...into the dustbin and then I'll be brave and put it in the garbage. I can do that. I can tie the garbage bag. Wait! Where are you going? Ohhh, ohh, I can't believe you're doing this all by yourself! Here, let me help. Oh, never mind. Good, you're doing real good. He's gone! Are you sure there aren't any more around? Thank you. Thank you so much.

I faced my phobia. I'm cured.

I did it! I really did it!

SCARED

A young man responsible for his friend losing his job at a prep school desperately tries to silence him.

Hey man, I didn't know. Look, I'm sorry. You're not going to say anything, are you? I mean to anybody...here. The honor code and all... I saw you talking to Professor Schwartz. You were both looking at me. What were you saying? Did I ever tell you about my parents? What they do? How they have sacrificed for me and still are to get me through law school? My poor mom works two jobs. She works in an office all day, and then, of all things, she goes to work as a maid cleaning businesses. Is that embarrassing or what? My dad...well, I never see my dad. He always works the late shift. Law school is their dream. Their son - - the lawyer!

I'm not asking you to do anything except to keep quiet. Remember, I asked you if getting me a discount was going to get you into any trouble and you said "no!" Look, if you have anything to do with getting me called up on the honor code, I don't know, it could be bad. For you. I've got plenty of friends, see? Plenty.

Look, I'm an honorable man. My honor is all I have in this school. So help me.

Wait. Come back! I don't know what I'm saying.

(Pause.) I'm scared, man. Who knew buying computers directly from the school at wholesale was illegal? Nobody wanted to get you fired. I know things got bad when I kept calling and coming by. The evil looks those women gave me. Hey, I'll give you money. You want money? I don't have a lot, but I could write an I.O.U. or something. I'll give you anything you want. Hell, I'll buy my honor if I have to! Nobody can find out.

Sorry...sorry...

SELF-WORTH

A young man new to the business world learns his worthiness, shares with a coworker.

I'm done. I'm done with feeling beaten down by life. I mean...that I am worth something. Ben, this stuff doesn't come easy to anyone. But after being with those self-centered egotistical jerks and watching them down giant shrimp and gossiping their heads off, I can say that I stood there and had a revelation! All of a sudden, they looked ridiculous. The big guy, what's his name, Jerome? *(Laughs.)* He spilled tartar sauce on his tie. What a slob! I'm sure that's a $200 designer tie, and he's standing there with a greasy smear on it. Those stains never come off ties, Ben. Never. But I felt exalted, felt this wave of worthiness sweep over me as I meandered around the room, silently mocking them, all of them, except for you, of course. I watched and listened to the "suits"...all their bull. I felt important. My name feels good to me. Don't laugh at me! Do you know what I'm talking about? After feeling like scum all my life and being told that I'm worthless, it's like I'm in the secret club! So as I stood there between that pasty bean pate and the cucumber sandwiches, I grew about five inches. No more will I look to others to justify my life. That's over. I wonder if they ever felt the same way I did - - worthless? Or have they also had this discovery? Does that mean that all the jerks are truly worthy themselves? That's confusing me. I don't know, Ben. We work for a company that chews people up and spits them out. That room full of so-called VIPs! Right. There was only one in there. Me! Now you can laugh.

TONY

A man is warding off a would-be boyfriend in his apartment.

Let me be very clear with you. I am not looking for a boyfriend. That space is gone for me right now, and I can't handle it. If that is what you are looking for, please look somewhere else. I just want a friend, a real friend. What are you doing? I just sat here and told you I didn't want a boyfriend, and you put your hand on my knee? What the "h" were you thinking? Nobody listens anymore. When I say, "let me be very clear," that means "let me be very CLEAR!"

Well, you've spoiled everything now. Look, I'm going to be moving to San Fran, and I certainly don't want to bring any extra baggage with me. Oh, don't take it like that. I'm financially bereft, I have no friends, especially since nobody will allow themselves to be just my friend, and I have no job. So I'm not exactly the world's best catch. My ex-boyfriend, Clayton, still loves me, and I have issues with him I'm still working out. It's private, alright? So, if you don't mind, I don't want to see you again.

My God! You kissed me! You just don't get it, do you? No, I won't be quiet. What is this, high school? NO, it won't all work itself out. Put your shirt back on and leave NOW.

Let me be clear about this. I hate you and never want to see you again. I'm seriously considering the priesthood because of you. Now get out!!

(Sigh.) I need a drink . . .

PART THREE:
SENIOR MONOLOGUES

HILDEGARDE DE BINGEN

A twelfth century mystic reveals her gift of visions from God. Start slowly with head bowed in prayer.

Amen.

(Looks up.) My name is Hildegarde de Bingen. I was born many years ago. I did many things...and yet, not enough. But then, I did so many things because there seemed to be several whole selves of my own self that wanted to come through me. This caused me great pain. There were days when my body ached, my spirit sank, frozen.

Then, of course there were the visions. Ah! How I saw things. The veil was lifted for me. I was pushed or pulled thru. I stood in the midst of such wonder. At times, I was actually within the very molecules, the sub-atomic spaces, entities of understanding, the physics, ah! I have no words. I was given a gift. Such a gift! God revealed himself to me in such glory, such unusual beauty. In plants, in architecture, in song, music, words, philosophy, medicine, science.

There is nothing that does not have our maker in it. His touch is life. Life is God. I was shown the greening, the life-force. There are worlds that I was shown that I have no words to describe. Words are finite, and I was shown infinity. Why me? This special dispensation to myself worried me much. Alone with all this. Trusted no one.

I think I made God angry. I'm sorry! I'm sorry for being so weak. I became so ill I was given a direct order from God to write, to share, to write. I made enemies within the church. Harsh critics. I had a good friend in a bishop who with his encouragement allowed me to do what I was bid. Oh, so you see, I had to write. Volumes. Painted hundreds of pictures trying to visually share what I had seen. How frustrating it was when my little mind could not aptly communicate what I had been shown. I was so loved. That, dears, is what I wish for you. That you could understand the incredible beauty of the human body and of the earth. And how the two are the same. True, there are wonders, but the most wondrous is the human body.

Love yourself, for God has revealed himself in you. *(Bows her head back down.)*

JUST THIS ONCE?

An elderly woman urges her very old and very sick husband to go ahead and die for convenience's sake.

Excuse me, do you have a minute? I just got off the phone with a dear relative, you remember Patricia, our daughter? Well, it seems I've upset the whole family because I told everybody that you were, well, not going to make it as of May. And, well, you see...here it is...November. And you're still here. Not convenient at all. This time I don't want people mad at me because you just won't die. So if it's not too much trouble, would you mind helping me out, just this once? It seems that Patricia and her husband had picked out a real nice 36" "mammoth wall-mounted plasma TV" with all the bells and whistles. You know, it has a videoplayer, a CD, a DVD player.

Anyway, it's got all the D's and some blue - - thing. There were plans for vacations to Acapulco and the like. I should never have told them how much money they were going to get. Oh well. Now, if you would just take a minute and think this thing through, I'm sure you would see my point of view. I don't want to get their hopes up again, and then, bang! There you are, still around. It's not for me, mind you, that I'm asking. I just hate to be put in the middle like this. They are all saying that it's my fault. Your being alive and all. It was the love, the food, the trips to the doctor. One meal too many, too much random kindness. Look. Be a sport. Go ahead and kick the bucket.

(He expires, she smiles.) **That's a dear.**

KING'S PIE

A rather harmless senior spokeswoman rambles during a commercial break...on the air, live.

Hi... Now here's a recipe for King's Pie. A delicious - - what? Say what? Ooohh, dear. I forgot. I'm suppose to announce the sponsor for this recipe break. Is this it? Okay. This recipe break is brought to you by "Choisee's Flour." Oh dear... I don't like their flour *(Speaking to producer.)*

It's too thick, becomes lumpy very easily in gravies, doesn't even sift well. No sirree. I wouldn't even have the empty bag in my home!

Now...let's see...where were we? Oh, yes. Hi... Now here's a recipe for King's Pie! It is right out of my old aunt Mabel's kitchen. Well, at least, I think it was Aunt Mabel. It could have been a recipe from that other woman who was staying with her for some ten-odd years. Weirdo. Smelled bad. Never quite sure which side of the bread she buttered on, if you catch my drift. Anyway, it is a good recipe. Although if it does comes from a deviant source, then I'm not so sure I should share. Nobody ever really shared anything with me when I was growing up. Oh, I could tell you stories. Whew! You'd never go back in a kitchen!

(Laughs.) What? Read the what?? Stop waving at me, and tell me what you want. You know, they hire these young whippersnappers right out of college, and they don't have any respect. Young man, you had better stop getting yourself in a tizzy! Hey - - what are you doing? Unhand me! Masher! Help me!! Heelllppp... What about the recipe? Heeeellllppppp!!!! *(She is dragged off the set.)*

LISTEN HERE

English matron at a social committee meeting at her retirement home demands all the attention to herself.

I was talking, if you don't mind. Very good. It's nice when everyone is polite. I'm now calling this meeting to order. Yes, Miriam? No, we are not discussing your son-in-law tonight. It's unsavory. Absolutely not. We accomplished nothing last week. Oh, please don't take offense, darling. It's time to move on. Now, the first piece of business has to do with the possibility of putting curry into the main dish on Friday nights. I for one, don't have a problem with Indian food. It's just that I don't want the whole place smelling like a foreign country. Not that there is anything wrong with a country that is not our beloved England. We are small but strong and forthright. Now, all in favor of curry, raise your hands. There, that's settled. We will have yellow food on Friday nights.

Item two. Our grand flea market. I have noticed that several of you have donated soiled items. This is not a pleasant thing to do. Nor is it sanitary. Think! Your little items reflect who you are in here. *(Pounds on her chest.)* Please, think. There. That's all I have. Does anyone have any important bit of news to share? Yes, Miriam? You just couldn't hold your tongue, could you? Alright. Somebody help her up. Oh, not that stupid business about the tablecloths again, is it? Well, it is stupid. Not your family, the tablecloths. **Cow!?**

Did everyone hear that she just called me a cow? Everyone remember that Miriam called me a cow. I don't want anyone to forget. I am a cow. She repeated it several times. Thank you, Helen, five times to be exact. I have been called a cow five times. I want it in the notes. Thank you.

MIRIAM'S COOKING SHOW

A strong-opinioned, frustrated, blathering cooking show host.

Hi, and welcome to Miriam's Cooking Show. Actually, I don't know why they call it Miriam's Cooking Show. It's not really Miriam's Cooking Show. For one thing, I've never even met Miriam. I don't even know if - - stop waving at me, I'm fine...if there even is a Miriam. Have you ever met a Miriam? Well, anyway, my name is Sylvia. So I don't know why they can't call it Sylvia's Cooking Show. Maybe it doesn't sound as good. What? Stop waving at me. It's my producer. Yeah, hi! I'm doing fine. *(Waves to him off the set.)* Okay. Today we are going to discuss making biscuits. Or...was it pound cake? Oh, dear... Well, what about we make pound cake out of biscuits? *(Laughs.)* I think I made a joke, but I'm not sure. Let go of my arm, I'm doing fine. My producer's a little antsy, I suppose. Antsy in his pantsy. I can remember when my mother used to say to me, "What? Do you have ants in your pants?" *(Laughs, pause.)*

You know, I never really knew what that meant. Do you know what that means? Anyway, ants don't have anything to do with biscuits or pound cake. So, first of all, do you have your aprons on, ladies? Oh, I'm sorry, I'm not suppose to say just ladies anymore. Ladies and gentlemen. Good, good. Is it tied real snug in the back? Don't tie it too tight, because it cuts off the circulation, and then sometimes I find my mind wanders when my apron is too tight.

(Her mind wanders, sings.) La-la-la-la...

What? You want me to stop? I think he's giving me the "Stop" gesture. You want me to stop cooking? Well, why do you want me to do that? We're on the air... Hi! What, what - - let go of me! No, let go! Well, I'll see you next week. Remember about the cookies or the biscuits or the ants or whatever!

Bye!

(She is being dragged off the set.) Gotta go! Unhand me! Where are we going?

WILD ONE

A 72-year-old woman explains why she's having the time of her life in Las Vegas to her 55-year-old daughter.

Uh-oh...it's the scornful look. What are you looking at, my halter top? I'm fillin' it pretty good, eh? So what if I'm wearing a dog collar. Ruff, ruff!! I LIKE IT! It's fun. I'm seventy-two years old, for God's living sake. That's right for LIVING'S SAKE! Just because you want to curl up and die at 55 doesn't mean that I have to die right alongside you. You and craggy old Ben. Well, I'm sorry, dear, but you could do much better. He has that "I'm about to die smell." I keep looking for a coffin when he's around. At least I have a musky strawberry-kiwi aroma around me. "Oh, Mom, come along with us to Las Vegas, the air will do you good." Well, the MEN have done me good. Do you have any idea what it's like to have men ogle you at my age? I don't care what part of my body they're looking at! At least they're looking! I've had a catharsis. **I'm alive!**

Which brings me to a point. Did I understand you right? The other night with dear Benjamin? Does he...brush his hair or his teeth ever? Anyway, I heard you. "What are we doing with all that money when she dies?"

Hello!! What do you think these are hanging here? Not my boobs! My ears! They're ears! And they work! I'd appreciate it if when you are planning my demise and how you're going to spend your inheritance you'd whisper next time. I'm sensitive.

I'M NOT DEAD YET!! I don't have to sacrifice anymore. No sirree...I'm footloose and fancy free, kicking up my heels in Las Vegas, Nevada and having the time of my life. Of course I don't kick as high as I used to. Look, I know I'm not Marilyn Monroe. I'm better.

I'm Bessie Teresa Briggs and I'm alive!

(Takes her daughter's hand, places it on her heart.) Feel that? It's still beating. Still. It beats. Over and over. What am I supposed to do with a life that keeps on going and going like that damn rabbit on the TV? There are still apples at the end of my branch, missy. I plan on reaching for them. If you're smart, you'll be right behind me.

Now, does this halter look good or not?

BACK TO SCHOOL

An older father who is returning to school looks to his middle-age son for approval.

You always had everything figured out, didn't you, Danny-boy? Where you were going, how you were going to get there and what you had to do to get there. Don't interrupt me. It's my time now. It's your father's time! Your old dad is different from you. I still don't understand how I made such a narrow-minded son. Okay, okay. This morning I registered at the community college, and I start Monday. At seventy-two years young, I want to learn something before I die. And your mother, God bless her soul, would be proud of me. Why can't you just support your ol' dad in this? Why can't you be proud of me? Humiliating??

This has nothing to do with you. So what if everyone in town knows the Attorney General's father is taking a few courses at Mid-East Tyler Community College. How in the world is that going to affect your precious reputation? I would think everyone would say education is great for the ol' man.

Look, I have my new satchel, fresh pencils - - sharpened and ready to go - - my three new notebooks. Even got one of those little zipper thingies. I've signed up for car mechanics and a speech class. Imagine me giving speeches! Hope carrying my books won't hurt my spine.

I know I haven't been the greatest dad in the world. Okay…I was pretty rotten. But that doesn't mean you have to be a rotten son. I need you to be proud of me, son, just this once. Tell me I'm doing the right thing. How much time do I really have left?

Ah, hell's bells. Look, the thing is, I'm nervous about Monday. I know I'm going to be the oldest student and even older than my professors. Will you…drive me, you know, my first day? Danny-boy?

CHOCOLATE KISSES

AUTHOR'S NOTE:
When I was a graduate theatre student, I volunteered at a medium security women's prison. During a break, I met this older gentleman in a quaint diner across the road from the prison and he offered me some Hershey's Kisses. Sitting there, drinking my coffee and looking out at the prison, the following character emerged.

A well meaning older man approaches two women at a table for simple conversation.

Here ya go. *(Gives the two ladies some chocolate kisses.)* You two look like ya could use a couple of sweets. I can't do sweets hardly anymore. Nope...used to be a time I could eat anything I wanted. But, well, now...nope, not anymore. You two look like you're all fussied up for something real special. Not much happens around here, except when they have some trouble up at the prison. Up the road. Ever been in there? I used to work there. No love in there. Naw, no...nothin' in there. It's a medium security joint, but they treat the women there like dogs.

You look 'em right in the face and there's nobody home. Yep, I used to work maintenance. Cut the lawns. Make everythin' look real nice. It's funny, don't ya think? They care more for the look of the grounds than they do for the souls of those poor women? Some of 'em'll scare you. Ya see, they look like men. That last law they laid down where all the women had to have their hair cut. Whew! That was bad. They cut more than their hair. They cut their "female" away. They say the manager or whoever it is that runs that place don't care for women. No, he don't care for criminals, either. Lock 'em up and throw away the key!

That's why I had to leave. You see, I did care for 'em. Yeah, I still care for 'em.

Well, you ladies enjoy your little chocolate kisses there. Some people...well, some folks don't ever get chocolate kisses. *(He saunters off slowly.)*

HONEY

AUTHOR'S NOTE:
I have an intimate relationship with the small seaside Texas town of
Galveston, Texas. My mother and her entire family were from Galveston.
My great-grandfather died by being hit with one of the thousands of pieces
of roof-top slate flying around in the great hurricane of 1900. This
monologue is a mixture of information I gleamed from the 1900 storm
museum in Galveston, several books I've read about the storm, and of
course, from my imagination steeped in my own family's tragedy. Play him
slowly, sincerely.

*An elderly man is haunted by his wife's drowning in the famed 1900 Galveston
flood.*

She was the most beautiful wife, almost celestial. Stars for eyes and long dark
hair you could get lost in. It was the howling wind that scared me. This was no
ordinary storm. I knew our beloved Galveston was going under.

Water started creeping under our front door. Our house was on 31st Street,
right on the shore. The shore. There was no more shore. Just wave upon wave
pounding our beautiful city. Took out all the electricity. The only light was
from the lightning when it lit up the sky.

Honey grew frantic about an elderly cousin of hers. She had to make sure she
was alright, she said. I grabbed her wrist and pleaded with her to stay inside safe
from the rising water. The last time I saw her, she was running down the
darkened flooded street. From nowhere, a big black monster of a wave crashed
into the side of our house, and from where I was standing, I saw her go under. I
was pulled down our chimney and into the water. When I came to, I was
holding onto part of a neighbor's bench. I thought it was a bench. To my
horror, I saw that it was my drowned neighbor, Alston. I was too exhausted to
scream. In the pitch dark.

I didn't mind dying. Just didn't want to die alone.

I still live near the shore. It's there that I see her. Haunting me, haunting the town; in every wave, in every woman's white dress, in the wind. Why don't the dead leave the living alone? Honey, I'm sorry, I'm sorry! The ocean didn't want me! I'm the one left. At least you're back with the stars...

VIOLIN

An eighty-something gentlemen reminisces about his daughter's talent.

There's not a lot to look forward to from here on, now is there? Or to remember, these days. Except the music. That day, that music, that violin. What a day. My daughter was only thirteen years old when she entered herself into a music contest at school. That stifling auditorium - - I sat there and waited. Contestants went up, good, bad. Then our D.J. went up. That's what she liked to call herself. A regular tomboy, that one. Her name was Diana. My wife loved mythology, and she thought it was chic to name our only child after a goddess.

Up until then I hadn't paid much attention to her. She walked out and took her place in the middle of the stage. All was quiet. D.J. lifted her instrument to her chin and played. Tremendous! She played that instrument as if she was the violin. I felt myself moving to the edge of my seat, afraid to look around for fear I would lose a second of her magnificent playing. If time is a flexible dimension and can indeed stand still, then by God, it stood still that day. Everyone in the audience was just swept away by her. The way she played, it was intense, focused, and so frenetic that I thought she might fly out of her skin, literally. D.J. wasn't just our daughter anymore. She joined or was joined by something grandiose. My child was part of the many layers of existence - - they say there are 11 dimensions, did you hear that? Her entire little body wrapped itself around the music, the notes, the spirit of the piece. All the shadows came out and mixed with the light. I became frightened. The energy created became bigger than she was. She didn't stop at one piece. No, she continued on playing, playing a Chopin, then a Mozart. Nobody stopped her. Nobody stirred! Nobody breathed. She was 13 years old.

(Laughs.) Yes. I remember that day, those few moments, that violin, the music and D.J. Through her talent, I got to look through the magic keyhole to enter a secret world, if only for a few minutes. Everything else is done and can go. But I'm holding on to that. I guess I'll live for a couple more years. Then on to the other ten dimensions.

WORDS, JUST WORDS

Nearing the end of his life, a frustrated composer feeling the emptiness of his life is left with only his words.

I've taken too much on... Where am I going? I'm being swallowed, swallowed up by the depths of my talent. I have no time. Oh God, I have no time. Give me just a little of your precious hour. Stop the clocks. Let my story be told! Bursting, I'm bursting. The strings of the violin and the concertos themselves sing out my pain, my isolation. Still the images and songs come! Where are the quiet ones to take me to the land of the light, the land of the dancers? Pressure closes in on me. Where do I turn? Is there no one to take this journey with me? Standing alone with only this damned-able longing to finish my work, to finish *something*. *(Pause.)*

My life must mean something or else all is lost. Family? Where is my family? Did I ever have one? Means nothing. Empty, we are a mere structure without spirit. Whatever spirit there is drags me down. Something gnaws at me, eats at me to be released, to soar. It is chained by so many hands clutching. Let me go!! Let me go!! If it means my death, then so be it. I'm ready. I think I've always been ready. Sing my song! Won't someone sing my song? Play my music? Let the notes themselves break free of their own structure. And then take me, Creator, with you. There has got to be a place where all makes sense. It will soon be over. I go then...

PART FOUR:
NEBRASKA-INSPIRED
MONOLOGUES

DUDETTE

An older woman tries her hand at getting picked up at a country bar in Nebraska.

Hey there. You. Yeah...you. How's it going, partner? I'll have another. My regular. You know what it is. MY REGULAR! You must've forgotten. Rum and coke, sonny!

(Looks around.) Easy there on the rum. Hardly any at all. Hey! Whooooaa there, buddy. That's enough. De-sist there. What are you trying to do, kill me? Coke straight up is just fine with me. Alcohol makes me funny. Not ha-ha funny, but "funny" nevertheless. That a fun word to say, nevertheless, just rolls off the tongue. Try it.

You're a bit tight, aren't you, fella? Look, I've got plenty of Coke back at the ranch. My abode. A-BODE! Where I hang my hat, if I had one! My hotel room! Geez, do I have to spell it out for you here? How's about you and I saddle up on over there and finish this leathery conversation?

But - - don't push me. I don't like that.

Gosh, what a dump this is, hot and stuffy. Of course, it could be me and my flashes again. You know, I have ventilation at my corral. Ya know what I mean? It's real cozy. There's vents.

Look, let's just cut through all this red tape. This here's the key to my door. I'm across the street in 16C. **Timberbeef Motel.** Can you remember that? 16C, not 15B or 14E, it's **16C**. Now, repeat that- slowly! I don't hear so well. Good. We could talk, or well, actually we could stir up some dust, if you catch my drift. You're not really connecting with me, are ya there, fella? Well, whatever...can't be picky.

There she is. *(Pushes her key toward him.)* I'm just going to giddy up on out of here now and gallop out that door. I'm leaving now. You trot on over soon afterwards.

16C.

Bring your manhood.

Spurs wouldn't be bad either.

Yahoooo!

FEUDING B & B-ER

Pouring tea for a B & B guest in a Victorian bed and breakfast in a small town in Nebraska.

Thank you. We think it's a lovely town, too. Nebraska is full of small towns, all with lovely parks. When Josef and I decided to buy a bed and breakfast, I went online, and voila! There it was, the most striking Victorian mansion - - I went running to Josef, and I said, "Oh, Josef, Josef, I found it, I found it!" God does work in mysterious ways, even through eBay.

Scone? Freshly made every morning. Are you sure?

(Pouts.) Well, bless you, anyway. Please pause with me. "He that partaketh…"

(Smiles.) Oh, her? She's not open all the time. I, on the other, am always here, always open. It's funny, you know, how the competitor *(Smiles sweetly.)* advertises that she has artwork featured in her bed and breakfast. That's a joke! These fine pieces of artwork you see here are all my mother's original paintings. You can't even see the little numbers.

She copied me! That's all there is to it. "Don't judge, lest you be judged…" But my, oh my, **that woman, THAT WOMAN…**

More tea?

Thank you, the china is from Lilliput. From a very expensive overseas catalogue. Very exclusive. I bought that online too - - they were having a sale. You see, joy is fleeting. And it gives me great joy to think that I have a very DISTINCTIVE AND RARE place here. The "You're in a Hallowed Place Bed and Breakfast" is my delusion, eh, I mean - - my dream! It's really a shame when people that don't even go to church currently can sit on a chamber of commerce in the very township where they own a business and blatantly send any lead, any tourist to their establishment and build up their tirade, I mean, trade, instead of being fair and Righteous and **JUST!** - - by spreading the prosperity out a bit - - like they should be doing as public servants of the people.

(Her social mask slipping now, angry.) We have repairs. We have bills. We have a right to the business as much as she does. Just look at the place! Those are REAL LACE CURTAINS from the Shamrock Country - - IRELAND!

(Straightens out the curtains.) But enough. It's just about enough. "You're in a Hallowed Place Bed and Breakfast" is on the market.

WE ARE NOT ALL ONE. THAT'S LIE, A DAMN LIE!!

It's a dog-eat, dog-eat, whatever, world and I am sick of this town not supporting me. So...she can just go ahead and flaunt her precious little B & B without any competition from me. Besides, it's the Christian thing to do.

More tea?

HERE I LIE

Middle-aged woman lies in snow, frightened at her fall from a speeding sled.

Here I lie. Dead? A mere mangle...are these my last thoughts?

(Gasps for air.) My last breaths? How did I get to this place, lying here in the frozen snow? Why did we move here? Children - - laughing. Damn. Why don't they stop laughing? Don't they see me? It's like I'm invisible. I'm in trouble. Oh God, I'm in trouble. Help me! Get help. Breathe. Breathe...

(Deep breaths.) Have I been a good mother...or a waste? Son, I can't hear you. What are you saying? I see your lips moving, but I can't make out - - I'm afraid!! Here I go. That was so silly of me, grown woman sledding down a hill, going over that stupid ramp. How foolish. Who did I think I was? Stupid woman.

When I was in the air, I knew I was in trouble. I'm heavier, I went faster, landed harder. Get Dad, quick, help me. I just want to go home. Take me home. Hot bath, my new tea, candles lit, flannel nightgown. From now on I'm going to act my age.

How scary.

LONELY GIRL

Troubled young woman tries to connect with others.

Hi. I didn't see you out there. You startled me. Not "Oh my God!" startled, but startled anyway. I don't normally like to talk to strangers. See my dress? I'm going to be a movie star, or at least make on to "Americana Idol." Yes, I am. Anyway, up here - -

(Points to her head.) - - I am. I could be. Maybe not a grand, great big star, but something shiny. Like in the night sky, all twinkling up there. I'd like for everyone to be looking at me, twinkling. Everyone look up and see me! See my great big...mess? Thousands of things mixed...I'm lost in there....and here...somewhere. I'm in here somewhere. When my stepfather used to hit me on the back of my head or put me into the shower with my clothes on, just for giving my opinion, it, well, went. It's got to be something important for me to be able to be seen and heard. But I will. If you would look at me like I'm important maybe, that would help.

I'm tired of looking over my shoulder all the time. I'm only a voice now, now wearing the only dress, that I have left. I could use some help. Did you come to help me? Really?

Hear the music? That's the planets singing, like Aristotle said. I surprised you, didn't I? How could a simpleton know about singing planets?

I'm spinning and singing, but no one sees me. If they did, then that must be what heaven is like.

No more hits. No more cold showers. No more mess.

ONE LAST DANCE

AUTHOR'S NOTE:
Again, in my state-wide tour of Nebraska, there was one bar that I visited during the day where I found no one except the barkeeper who was cleaning up. Like any saloon visited in the middle of the day, it smelled of stale smoke and dried beer, but as I sat at the bar on a well-worn wooden swivel seat, I closed my eyes, heard the music and laughter, and felt the presence of this older woman. I saw her walk in, I saw her walk up to an old flame, and I heard her. It was in an old town where last chances and last dances seemed to go together. I, for one, hope she got that last dance in Anywhere, Nebraska. Now you, kind actress, let her live!

Elderly woman in Basset, Nebraska expresses her desire for one last dance with an old friend at a friendly neighborhood bar. She takes a swig of something and starts in…

I'd do anything to just have one last waltz with you, Teddy. But my legs, hell, they're no good. My hands, well, look at 'em! Like claws. Both knees have been replaced, every tooth in my darn head is either capped, pulled or done fell out. My toes have relations with the   cornfields. *(Laughs.)* Hell, I don't walk anymore, I shuffle. I'm so broken up that there are some days, weeks, I feel lost.

But on other days, good days, ya know, Teddy, I feel, well, different. Free, sort of. All this breaking down and rebuilding has made me realize that I'm no different from the farm I've worked all these years. I'm just somethin' else that falls apart after a while. This thing, this body, well, it's not me, the **me** I feel in those wee hours of the night. You know exactly what I'm talking about. Those hours when we wait for death.

When it's all said and done, that's all we all are, just parts of something bigger than us. When our parts can't be fixed anymore, and they're damn well hammered, like a fence that won't stay up, then you're forced to look at what's been important and what's of no use.

So here goes…

You may be someone else's husband, but you've always been my true love. My one friend. You may be wearing the most worn-out cowboy boots, plaid pants, a turquoise shirt and a tie that I don't even want to know where it came from, but you're still beautiful to me.

($looks at her worn leather gloves.) I've worn these leather gloves for ten years, got 'em in Omaha, had 'em shipped to me. Vanity - - couldn't stand the sight of my ugly and crippled…they've been my constant companions.

We used to waltz together, Teddy.

Well, it's been long enough.

(She takes her gloves off.) Give me your hands, you ol' coot. No need to hurry. Time's done all that for us. I would just give anything to have one last waltz with you.

Only one.

WINDMILLS' LESSON

AUTHOR'S NOTE:

This was my first Nebraska-inspired monologue that I wrote on my "Nebraska Speaks" tour sponsored by the University of Nebraska at Kearney, where I worked. First stop, Compton, Nebraska, the home of over 100 windmills (they say!) Arriving in mid-May, it looked pretty deserted, save some repairmen who let me in to see the house and windmills from a higher level. Sitting and looking out a window in an upstairs northeast bedroom, I awaited my inspiration. Windmills, inspire me! Sure enough, they did. First thing I got was a glimpse of a dirty, torn apron and deeply-lined hands from working too much. Finally, I heard this farmer's wife's lament. It wasn't hard to hear her. I just got out of the way and let her speak. Like all of us who work hard and look for that day when our "ship will come," this is a monologue that should speak to everyone.

A middle-aged woman, exhausted, shares her disillusionment with life with realtor.

I'm **so damn tired** of feeling melancholy. All the time. It's like a heat wave beating you down, down, down. I'm tired of hanging my head so low I wish someone would step on it like a melon.

The oldest child of six siblings, it was up to me to be an example. When I first started seeing Fred, I thought, hey ol' gal, your life is picking up, really going somewhere. The world is your oyster. I was going to be a farmer's wife. Wear nice store-bought cotton dresses, aprons, plant a little garden for myself, raise children, laugh a lot, laugh…everyone would be so proud of me, look up to me.

After the first hard winter, the cotton dresses turned into dirty overalls. The aprons did indeed stay and became as torn and stained as my dreams did. Fred was not my knight in shining armor. He was pure armor. Well, he had to be, didn't he? To survive? Then the armor started to crack and finally disintegrated. I stopped laughing. Still got the laugh lines though to prove I did laugh. See 'em? I suppose we're not supposed to be happy. Do you think that means we're not supposed to be happy? That it's not a God-given right?

But I'm tired, you see. Just so tired of all of it. I was patient, I waited. The ship never came in, after all these years. You see, I think I finally realized that I am the ship, the captain, the knight in shining armor, the dream itself. You see these windmills, turning, turning, turning, they never go anywhere but keep moving. They are me, and I am them. But no more. If you sit here on this porch and stare out at those 100 giant windmills, you can almost hear the siren's call towards beautiful possibilities, possibilities for me.

That's why I'm selling the place. Lock, stock and barrel. Maybe I'll leave the barrel. So the windmills will remember me and turn for me.

(Small laugh.) **A remnant of the dream.**

THE BROOM MAN

AUTHOR'S NOTE:

In historic downtown Omaha, there was an actual older half-blind gentleman who sold homemade brooms for years. Everyone just called him the Broom Man. He struck a chord in my heart immediately. He was a very interesting and courageous man. He'd strike up a conversation with anyone. A good soul, but down on his luck, here he has to handle several disappointments at once.

An elderly man, half-blind, frail, struggles to pick up his brooms after he's broadsided by a car.

Aaaaahhhhh, ooohhhh, I'm down!!

(Moans, reaches for his legs.) Are they, they broken? Are they - - alright? Yeah, yeah, okay, everything's okay. Didn't see that coming, 'course, I wouldn't, would I? Where am I? Where are they? Are they all here? Help! Anyone there? Help me! I can't see, not very well, not with these clouds over my eyes. Anyone?

I can't see. My brooms, there's four of them. I need all of 'em. All I got, ever…

(Gropes to find strewn brooms.) Here's one yep, here's two.

(A stranger comes and helps him collect his brooms.) Oh, thank you, thank you for helping me. Who are you? Just a passerby? Most people do pass me by. I'm the Broom Man. I'm Henry.

(Slowly stands up with help.) Thank you, thank you very kindly. If you could just point me in the direction of the corner, there by the fountain. That's home for me. You see these brooms? I sell 'em. I eat because of these here brooms. Because of my mamma and these brooms. She taught me how to make 'em. The whisk brooms are $5 and the larger brooms here are $12 apiece. All handmade by these hands. Any blood on them? Just don't want to get anything on the merchandise here.

(Stranger has to leave.) Naw, I understand. Well, thanks anyway for helping an ol' man. Wait, wait, come back. I'd like to give you one of my brooms. Take it, take it!

(Another stranger comes and takes the offered broom and runs away with it.) Hey! What are you doing? You're not the one who helped me. Help! Help! Someone please, stop him. He stole one of my brooms! Help!

(Sits in disgust and failure.) Stolen. Just like my eyes. I'm the Broom Man. My name is Henry. Brooms for sale!!! Brooms…always for sale.

Anyone?

DENNIS' PLEA

After his father's death, a young man returns with his new wife to his family's ranch in the beautiful Nebraska.

I hated it that he died in a hospital. He wanted to be buried out here. Where he lived, he wanted to die. He loved this land, his Golden Spires. Pops loved the fresh air, he died with tubes coming in and out of him. He used to laugh all the time. He cried at the end. He worked this land since he was a toddler, every day alongside his brothers and sisters and neighbors, good weather and bad. Tornado threats, ice storms, snow drifts, didn't matter. He was out in it. It was a part of him.

So, you see, you're asking me to do a lot. To leave this ranch, means to leave my Pops. I thought, you know, I hoped, I, that you *knew* who I was, I mean, at the core. Hon, look at me! I'm not a banker, I'm not a teacher, I'm not - - what am I wearing? Answer me that, then, what am I wearing? That's right, I'm wearing a suit right now because I just buried my dad, but underneath, what am I really wearing? Overalls! What was I wearing when you met me? Overalls!

Hell, I'm a rancher. My daddy was a rancher, my granddaddy and his daddy before him. My ancestors homestead this place. Do you know what that even means? They came out here with nothing, absolutely nothing except a love of the land along with a song and prayer. That's what my mamma always used to say. It wasn't easy for them - - any of them. My family's sweat and tears are all over this land. Golden Spires Ranch beat all odds out here. My grandma kept diaries. It tears me up to read them sometimes.

See over there, look, it used to be two barns were there, right over the ridge. That "black monster" as Grandma used to call it, took it and three cows - - almost took her, back in 1913.

Please, don't walk away from me. For God's sake, Frances, we want the same things. YES, WE DO! You want a beautiful place to live and bring up our child. Here it is!

(Difficult to say.) I've got dues to pay, hon...

There was always this unspoken understanding that I'd take over. I wasn't as good a help to him, to my pops as I could have been. I've got to do it now, I need to do it out of...love...for, for him, for Pops. I can almost hear him screaming at me not to abandon it - - him, her, the land.

It's payday, and I've got to do the paying.

Are you with me?

FOLLOW ME

AUTHOR'S NOTE:
After visiting a lot of Nebraska museums, I found myself watching a blind man as he was visiting the Scottsbluff Historical Museum. He seemed to enjoy listening to everyone around him remark about the various exhibits. When you act this monologue, it is important to physically give August a different center of energy or space when his thoughts are being articulated by the spirits talking to him. This can be a haunting monologue. August is a strong man who is blind but has a dream to make himself useful to his world.

August, a blind man tries to convince the curator of a Nebraska Museum he'd make a good tour guide as the museum's spirits intrude on his thoughts.

But I assure you - -

(Curator sneezes, August reaches for Kleenex and hands it to curator across his desk.)
- - bless you! You're welcome - - I just got over a cold myself.

I'm quite serious. The answer to your first question is that I'm a lover...of history, all history, except for mine of course.

(He touches his eyes.) BOLDNESS HAS GENIUS IN IT.

I've thought a lot about this.

A tour guide, you're thinking, a blind man? He must be crazy.

BUT IT'S MY DREAM.

I've one very good sense, that's listening. I hear things. You wouldn't believe what I hear. Sometimes I feel it's the very walls reaching out, the invisible to the invisible.

LOIE ROYCE WAS HER NAME. SHE HATED HER NAME.

I brought my tape recorder.

(Getting a little desperate.) Tapes, you see, I could listen to the tapes I make and I could memorize all the different stories, I'm already familiar with almost all the different sections in the museum.

TO LEAD WITH CONTRIBUTION.

These windows to the soul don't open any more. But oh, the jokes'r on me for I still see, I still get to, can't get away from, all the things I see. Wisps of people, like wind, they pass by me, circle me, I see them over there, feel them, sense them. They come to me. They follow me.

LOIE ROYCE WAS JUST A CHILD HERSELF, SHE WAS BLINDED BY THE SNOW AND LOST HER GRIP ON HER LITTLE WARDS.

They need me. Don't you see how much I have in common with them? A museum doesn't have to be about dust and death.

ONCE HER STORY IS TOLD SHE CAN BREATHE AGAIN THROUGH THE FROZEN GROUND AND FIND THE LITTLE ONES SHE LOST THAT MISERABLE COLD WINTER AFTERNOON.

Okay! *(To spirit).* I can be a human bridge, you see, for what you want to tell here. All these dead folk want me here. To tell their stories, so that their lives mean something. They follow me now.

IF YOU HAVE A DREAM, PURSUE IT.

Please, sir, let me do something good, be a benefit, not a drain.

I could be a leader!

(Starts to leave, stumbles.) I'll see myself out.

(To the spirits.) **FOLLOW ME.**

LONELY GUY

AUTHOR'S NOTE:
This piece was inspired by a performance piece originally created by Dan Jones. It was performed in an evening of original work at the University of Nebraska at Kearney entitled <u>Innovations,</u> which I directed. The "Lonely Guy" monologue was very touching. The singing interspersed with the text helps the pathos.

Lonely man strikes up conversation while buying frozen icicles.

Yes, I'll take those. Excuse me, excuse me, please. There are blue ones in there, aren't there? Because you see, it's very important...for me...you see, that there are blue ones in there. Blue is my favorite color. There are lots of important things that are blue. The "Blue Danube," "Blue Moon"...

(Sings a few bars from "Stardust.") STARDUST MEMORIES, THE MEMORIES OF LOVE'S REFRAIN...

There's no blue in that song. Except for the feeling, you see. It's got a blue feeling. That's what I am all the time. A shocking color of blue. Not navy or light baby blue, but a deep rich turquoise blue. Like the ocean. I like that. You're thinking, what does he want, this blue man with his frozen icicles?

I'll tell you what I don't want. I don't want to walk down the street or into a store and be <u>invisible</u>. Hey, you could do it. Just a friendly "hi, how are you?" every once in a while. Nothing deep. Nothing personal. I wouldn't ask for anything...anything more than not being invisible.

Please, where are you going? I didn't mean any harm in it...promise.

(Looks in carton.) There's no blue ones in here.

(Walks off singing "Blue Moon" lightly.) I SAW YOU STANDING ALONE, WITHOUT A CARE OF YOUR OWN...

LIVE WIRE

AUTHOR'S NOTE:
The story of this young thespian is true, from the annals of Brownville Village Theatre, a wonderful quaint church- made into a theatre in the small village of Brownville, Nebraska. Its history is rich with stories. As a guest director for a couple of summers there, I learned about this most unfortunate death that occurred during the time they were settling the church to its new location. Cut off from life too soon, here James gets his final say.

A young man tells of his last moments at a regional theatre in Nebraska.

He was a freshman, no - - a rising sophomore. It was summer 1973. It was really humid that summer. At his first professional audition, he was nervous. Of course he could sing and dance, and yes! He'd love to do tech - - learn new things...but - - why not?! He'd never heard the word "gofer" before. Moving a 100-year old church to a new location to become a theatre was awesome. So many possibilities.

Why was that wire live?

Why didn't anyone check it?

"James, scramble up there and see if you can straighten the steeple a little. Patch it while you're up there."

"No problem!" Scramble he did. Sure did.

If only he could get a little bit closer...just move the ladder over just a tad. So he did. As he was leaning over, the entire universe froze. The leaves stopped moving. The wind didn't exist. His story was about to take an abrupt, electrifying transformation.

(Desperate.) Mom?

Dad?

There was no one…to help him. There was an electric line, telephone line, whatever, that came to the top of the theatre from the main poles on the side of the road. Stretched across you see, like this. *(He demonstrates.)*

In one horrific nanosecond, the line, the hot line touched his ladder- his very aluminum metal ladder. James didn't remember flying or hitting the ground. Like a piece of burned toast, he crumbled into the dirt. All he remembered was standing up and saying,

"I'm okay! I'm alright!"

Then everything went out, complete darkness. No breath, no nothing. A final blackout. He… He…

I got some curtain call.

ODE TO AL

The spirit of a troubled man in his prime - - who took his own life - - tries to make sense of what he's done.

Why did I do it? Why not? Going to work everyday, working the labyrinth, that underground hellhole. Who would want to wake up everyday and know that's where they were going to work? The bending over, the neck pain, the loneliness, the lack of thanks. Are we just invisible people? Us who tread the facilities boards.

I always had a smile, but it came as a mask covers up an empty vile. Now, you wail and gnash your teeth. I'm just another reflection of the entire world. I don't want to be in a world of war, in a freezing destitute town where rapists get away scot-free and people die from spinning their stupid trucks out of control. The story about the young teenage girl who lost her life because a drunk driver was going the wrong way on the highway haunted me.

I've been going the wrong way for most of my life. My good looks didn't take me on that golden journey. Nothing but blackness filled my days and terror filled my nights. Girlfriend, family and friends have all turned on me. Or so I thought.

So here I am on the other side, wondering if I did the right thing. Now I see it all, so clearly. There is no right way to live, there's just the right to live. And I gave it up.

Aaaahh!!. So now my agony starts anew.

Jesus, if you can hear me, come get me. Please. I've no body to cry with, I'm only ethers of the universe. Please. Let me be reunited once more. I still feel the loneliness. Kiss all goodbye for me. I have no lips.

RANCHER'S THOUGHTS TO HIS CATTLE

AUTHOR'S NOTE:
As I drove through the beautiful Nebraska Sandhills and spotted herd after herd of cattle, I wondered if a rancher out alone with them ever gave his job a serious pondering. Here this one does.

A hard-working rancher in the western part of Nebraska rides his land, talks to his cattle.

Go on, git, git, git on! Damn. Damn. Damn. I'm doing a rancher's job, dress like one, talk like one, talk to you! In the end, what am I, huh? Don't look at me like that! Going along like everyone else in my family. Just going along like a little doggie, with everyone, everything. But you don't care do you? You don't even know what I'm talking about, "crazy human."

(Looks out over his fields and cattle.) Cattle. "Don't treat me like cattle." Who came up with that word anyway? You graze, you wander, you move. You chew. I graze, I wander, I chew. You look at me with those dark scary eyes as if you hate me because you know what you're being raised for. Dang. You make me feel uncomfortable. Well, you do.

(Shudders.) Are we all going to have to pay for this? And if so, will you eat **us**? I want to go. I need to stay. AAaaagggghhh!! My whole life, job after job, looking after you stupid cows. Don't be offended, you don't even know what that word means. Or do you? I'm just following the well-worn rut in the ground, you know, like a blueprint for my life. I don't remember agreeing to any of this. Living and working here in Nebraska surrounded by miles and miles of corn and wind that cuts through you like a knife. Oh…sorry.

Maybe there's not much difference between us, except that I can think ahead to the future and suffer because of that. If you knew what was coming, you'd be in agony. LISTEN, you, you! I'm done here, alright? I'm ready for my next step - - whooa, whooa. Look, whatever you do, don't come back as a 'me' - - as a person. Come back as something else. Or don't come back at all. I think I'll become a vegetarian. Okay, I'm a liar. You're lucky you don't know where you're going. I know, and it's nowhere. Hey! Don't turn your backside to me!

TRAINS A LOT

Ola-timer sits in his car watching the trains in Kearney, Nebraska, reminisces with his dead uncle about days gone by.

165 trains a day, ya say? Hey! That there's a long one. My uncle, the railroad man. A train engineer. I can still smell you, coming home to Grandma's wearing your conductor overalls.

(Takes a whiff of air around him.) That train smell. You and your secret room. Did you know Grandma would never let us kids in there when you were away working? I'm sorry for pestering you every time you stepped into the door. "Uncle Bobby, let me wear your hat, let me put on your gloves. Whoo-oo-whoo!!" *(Laughs.)* I'm sure you were exhausted and didn't want little kids hanging on you. You were such a giant of a man. Did things with your life. Don't know if you'd be too much proud of me. Went from job to job. Heck, I've had about as many jobs as there are trains here. I started out good. Did you know I wanted to be a railroad man like you, Uncle Bobby? I wish we could just all go back and live at Grandma's again. Do you know what I remember most about her house besides your darn secret room? The enclosed stairs going up to her attic. Sis and I could see miles of Nebraska farmland from her attic. We'd watch out for you to come home, watch the cranes fly in each spring. That was our secret room...where we dreamed. 40, 42, 43, 44, 45.

Hey, what was in your room that was so secretive anyway? It can't matter now. "You kids stay away from Uncle Bobby's room!" Grandma used to yell at us. Locked door, overalls, leather gloves, dirty conductor's hat. You always seemed to go out and live life. Home for seven days, gone for 14.

I have a confession to make. You know sis and I always wanted to see what was behind that locked door. One morning, we got a hairpin from Grandma and tried to pick the lock. Then just as we were about to open it, we both had an overwhelming feeling of doing wrong. Guess we'd been brought up too well. We never did try and open your room again. I think we figured out that a man's got a right to privacy, if nothing else.

Uncle Bobby? Count with me? 78, 79, 80, 81.

(Beat as he continues to watch the trains go by.) It didn't matter that you weren't my real uncle. You were real enough to me. I'm like these trains here, going this way and that way, and never really going anywhere. I'm at the end of my track. Uncle Bobby, if you can hear me, please come pick me up...wearing your conductor's overalls. Don't forget the gloves. Take me home. 163, 164, 165...

VALENTINE'S SON

AUTHOR'S NOTE:

After receiving a small grant to tour Nebraska and visiting many museums, I asked the curator at the Valentine Museum in Valentine, Nebraska if they had any interesting stories connected with any of their items. At first she said no, I turned to leave, and then she said, well, there was this one fellow who was handicapped and we ended up with all those beautiful kerosene lamps there. The result is giving this intriguing man his due. I immediately knew I had to call it Valentine's Son.

A physically challenged older man tries to understand why his beautiful collection of glass lamps and dishes were taken from him.

Everything is changing. I don't - - anything to change - - I don't want anything to change. They've taken my things, ya know…all my beautiful things. The old kerosene lamps with the huge painted roses on them. Those soft roses that loved me? I know they did. They accepted me, twisted limbs and all. I know - - hey! did you ever get a chance to look at 'em? Gosh, I started collecting way back…it all started back when…electricity stole our lives. The women, they're the wasters, the ones - - they just threw everything away, threw out those kerosene lamps.

Hey! Do you remember the soft light? Everyone slow down! Mama and me sitting by the soft yellow light from yesterday. Like the moon.

I knew better, didn't I? Wasn't I the one who knew better? To see beauty for what it was, lying there next to yesterday's garbage? Kinda like me, nobody ever saw me. Just saw my affliction. But! I took them. I took them all. People said I hoarded them. I didn't care. I loved them. All the pretty drawings on the lamps, on the dishes, the flowers, the leaves, the gold. I loved the gold. Everyone needs someone to care about them, to see their beauty.

They spoke to me because no on else would. People were afraid of me. Said I was crazy.

My days? Oh they were filled with collecting them, cleaning them, polishing them. I'd sit for hours you know, talking to a lamp as if we were both in a fancy ranch and I was perfect, you know, my body. Forty years of collecting: 450 gas lamps, over 1000 plates and dishes. They were my friends. They told me I was their hero because I saved them from the wasters. We were a family. They didn't care I couldn't walk right or talk very well.

But Ma got sick. She got sick, didn't she? Why did you have to die? Mammaa?? Don't you know what they've done? They've taken everything from me. Had a huge sale with lots of people touching them, feeling them, MY THINGS!! Dirty strangers with dirty hands, no respect, just took 'em away.

The government men said I could pick out the best ones, but not for me, to put into some kind of museum, there in the town. Said I could visit them. Why did everything have to change? Why couldn't I keep my beauty?

(He is being called for by a nurse.) Alright, I'll be right there. I have to go take my medicine before I get, well…really upset.

(Turns to go.) Oh, I hope you got enough for your story. I'm not too interesting.

(Shuffles off.) Everything changes…

PART FIVE:
ALASKA-INSPIRED
MONOLOGUES

MOOSE SCRAPBOOK

New tourist cyclist in Alaska hiding in bushes rambles about frustration of being afraid of running into a moose.

Ssshhh! What's that?? You know what makes me so ding-dong angry? MOOSE - - at least the idea of moose, the very thought of moose - - here I am, breathing in the beautiful new day, ready for a jaunt into the sun - - that never goes down - - by the way - - and why the HELL doesn't the sun go away, go down?? It's not natural, it's not normal. It's not right.

Anyhoo, back to my moose "issue." Is that an antler - - no, just a branch. Sorry, I'm a bit nervous here. Okay, so here I am, I'm outside, have slithered my fat body into this sleek black rider's outfit complete with matching gloves and helmet, and I crouch here, behind a giant fir, frozen with fear, hands glued to the handlebars, feeling like a human target.

Oh, Moose!! I just know you are out there, a herd of you...waiting for me. I can hear them snorting and making clandestine clever pithily plans to angrily ambush me. I hear the mother moose encouraging her little moose brood to delight in their first cycle-scare. She's been taking scrapbooking lessons and already has a page laid out to chronicle the big beastly event. All she needs is a 5x7 glossy of her little darling scaring the heebie-jeebies out of an unsuspecting cyclist. That would be me.

THEREFORE, I HEREBY DECLARE: THERE WILL BE NO MERRIMENT ALONG THE TRAIL TODAY. NO-HO!

I have to turn tail once again, because of the hidden enemy #1. Moose – I HATE THEM.

Let's move out.

MOOSE ANYONE?

Sitting as a passenger in a native Alaskan's van, a new tourist in Alaska shares frustration about some of the advertised pull to visit Alaska.

Another moose sign! Oh right, TAKE THAT SIGN DOWN! It's all an ugly lie - - a trap, a clever marketing ploy to get tourists to come to Alaska - - and I'm not buying it.

THERE ARE NO MOOSE IN ALASKA!

And don't even get me started about the bears. I've not seen one frickin' bear except on napkins and bank logos since I've been here in my entire four weeks. Yeah, I came here for a two-week stint, and I've ended up staying for four. *The Last Frontiersmen* have trapped me here, like a dog, like a prairie-dog. I've fallen into a traveler's black hole - -

except!

for the fact that the sun never goes down. I guess it was the lure of the snow-capped Heidi-running up the mountain scenery, the singing waterfalls - - which I'm beginning to suspect are all done with mirrors - - and the "free" salmon that just flops onto your plate. Well, absolutely none of it's true. It's a lie, a lie, a lie.

Ooooohhhh!! PULL OVER, Pull over, pull over.

(Sings.) "The hills are alive." **CAMERA! CAMERA!**

(Snaps a picture.) Aaahhh, **Alaska,** "the other white meat."

Hey! That moose stole my camera! Stop!!

PART SIX:
FORMLESS SCENES

INTRODUCTION

Formless scenes, also known as content-less scenes, are simple, one-line scenes that can be used for theatre (acting, directing and design) classes, auditions and rehearsal techniques. Actors have to fill in all the blanks; create their own setting and relationships, figure out the blocking, who is talking, the situation, the conflict, and the resolution, etc. The words are all you have. It's a chance to be both actor and playwright as well as director!

These sixteen short "scenes" are quite original and propose a challenge for even the most experienced actor. Have fun with them - - sing them, dance them, 200% overact them, mime them or plain old "act them." Whatever you, your partner(s) and/or your acting teacher/director decide to do with the scene, experiment and have fun. Also, search out the subtext - - what's really going on - - when appropriate.

These scenes are great for teaching, directing, and even for a design student. Consider exploring different acting styles or theatre genres. If the genre is to be a farce taking place in a barn, it is quite different from taking the same scene as a tragic drama and setting it the day after a married couple learns they can't have children, etc. Since there is no playwright dictating exactly what the given circumstances are, you the actor have to supply all the before moments, the life behind the words and the environmental conditions of the scene. Lots to do with such a simple scene!

Sample Settings:
Psychiatric Hospital
Church
Master Bedroom
Kitchen
Desert
Mansion
Boss' s Office

Morgue
Wedding
Funeral
Laundromat
Swamp
Barn

Sample Relationships Between Characters:
Siblings
Patient/Doctor
Employee/ Boss
Mother/child
Teenager/Mother
Teenage Lovers
Friend/Enemy
Family Members
Strangers
Melodramatic Heroine/Hero
Tragic Figures
Historical Figures
Famous People
Nurses/Doctors
Therapist/Client

Sample Conditions:
Friends after a silly fight
Lovers the next morning
Parents struggling to stay together
Co-workers vying for the same job
Mental Patients hiding
New lovers embarrassed the morning after
Doctor testing a patient
Married couple role-playing

Children being very naughty
Cross-dresser with straight sibling

Other Ideas:
Even though a lot of these formless scenes are written for two actors, experiment having a chorus, being an inanimate object, becoming part of the scenery, reaching for an abstract portrayal of an emotion, or even splitting the lines up amongst several actors. Some lines can be repeated like a refrain in a song, others can be whispered, shouted or sung.

To play these pieces and still be in the moment, make vigorous, dangerous choices to challenge you and your partner. Take us all on an emotional journey. Make strong and dynamic physical choices as well as emotional and intellectual ones. Remember, bold acting choices usually have something to do with human relationships, violence or money. Go for it. It is the spirit behind the words that sell any scene. Live that.

SCENE ONE

SPEAKER 1: What's that in your ear?

SPEAKER 2: Don't come any closer.

SPEAKER 1: I said something to you, are you deaf?

SPEAKER 2: I'd be careful if I was you.

SPEAKER 1: Looks like a banana.

SPEAKER 2: I love bananas!

SPEAKER 1: Is everybody here bananas?

SPEAKER 2: Not me, I'm a peach.

SPEAKER 1: This is all so fruity. Ha. Ha. Ha.

SPEAKER 2: I'm very - - very curious about you.

SPEAKER 1: So, what the hell is in your ear?

SPEAKER 2: It's not an ear- - look closer, my dear.

SPEAKER 1: My gosh! You're an alien!

SPEAKER 2: Affirmative.

SPEAKER 1: Beam us all up then.

SPEAKER 2: What's happening?

SPEAKER 1: We're going up on a super nova spaceship.

SPEAKER 2: Hold on!

SPEAKER 1: Zzzzssshhhh!!!

SCENE TWO

SPEAKER ONE: There you are, I love you so.

SPEAKER TWO: Who are you?

SPEAKER ONE: I've been looking for you all my life.

SPEAKER TWO: Where have you been looking?

SPEAKER ONE: I'm Dana, and I've been here waiting all the time.

SPEAKER TWO: What? I'm Dana.

SPEAKER ONE: Who's Dana?

SPEAKER TWO: Wait a minute. I'm very confused here.

SPEAKER ONE: Just listen for a one second.

SPEAKER TWO: Ha! Take that!!

SPEAKER ONE: All of you people, you - -

SPEAKER TWO: I resent that.

SPEAKER ONE: Well, the truth is, we all need someone to love us.

SPEAKER TWO: Do you work for Hallmark or something?

SPEAKER ONE: Anyway, I'm still Dana.

SCENE THREE

SPEAKER ONE: It's this way. It's our heritage

SPEAKER TWO: The storm won't let us get through that. You know that.

SPEAKER ONE: If we work together, it can work. It's got to work.

SPEAKER TWO: I wish Joey hadn't died.

SPEAKER ONE: Many will die. Many will, I'm afraid.

SPEAKER TWO: If we can get up this hill, we'll have done a lot.

SPEAKER ONE: I think the wind is dying down. Let's go now.

SPEAKER TWO: That's a positive attitude. I like you for that.

SPEAKER ONE: I wish Joey hadn't died. We're all going to die on this mountain.

SPEAKER TWO: If we have to go, we have to go.

SPEAKER ONE: No. I'm not going.

SPEAKER TWO: She's right, I'm not leaving either.

SPEAKER ONE: Well, I suppose this place is not any worse than any other.

SPEAKER TWO: I'm too young to die. I'm too young to die.

SPEAKER ONE: You can already smell death.

SPEAKER TWO: Let's sing, sing our national song, so we'll remember, til the end.

SCENE FOUR

SPEAKER ONE: We can't keep meeting like this.

SPEAKER TWO: No one knows.

SPEAKER ONE: No one cares.

SPEAKER TWO: You got that right.

SPEAKER ONE: I'm just so tired of all this.

SPEAKER TWO: You're wearing the shirt.

SPEAKER ONE: Yes, I thought it would make you - -

SPEAKER TWO: Happy?

SPEAKER ONE: Yes.

SPEAKER TWO: Well, guess again.

SPEAKER ONE: We'll do more than that.

SPEAKER TWO: You know me too well.

SCENE FIVE

SPEAKER ONE: Oh my God, did they hear us?

SPEAKER TWO: That's just great.

SPEAKER ONE: Now what?

SPEAKER TWO: Hide.

SPEAKER ONE: That's ridiculous.

SPEAKER TWO: Grown people, hiding, it is funny.

SPEAKER ONE: If we don't, then it's all over.

SPEAKER TWO: Who says?

SPEAKER ONE: They do.

SPEAKER TWO: Just stay close to me, and then we'll be free.

SPEAKER ONE: We'll never be free.

SPEAKER TWO: Shhhhh!!

SCENE SIX

SPEAKER ONE: If I get the job, we'll have to move.

SPEAKER TWO: Not again!

SPEAKER ONE: It's too cold here.

SPEAKER TWO: And you don't mean the weather, do you?

SPEAKER ONE: Look at me.

SPEAKER TWO: I'm looking.

SPEAKER ONE: Not really.

SPEAKER TWO: I'm looking.

SPEAKER ONE: You've never really seen me at all.

SPEAKER TWO: I gesture a lot.

SPEAKER ONE: A piece of art is a gesture.

SPEAKER TWO: So, are we moving or not?

SPEAKER ONE: I might go alone.

SPEAKER TWO: Go, then.

SPEAKER ONE: Come with me.

SPEAKER TWO: Love me?

SPEAKER ONE: Gestures and all.

SPEAKER TWO: You do love me.

SCENE SEVEN

SPEAKER ONE: We can drive straight through. It's over there.

SPEAKER TWO: There's a frickin' tornado heading this way. Are you crazy?

SPEAKER ONE: We'll be fine. Remember we have guardians looking out for us.

SPEAKER TWO: Grandma lost her house in a twister.

SPEAKER ONE: Please, not that again.

SPEAKER TWO: She was my only true friend.

SPEAKER ONE: You really know how ruin things.

SPEAKER TWO: I don't mean to.

SPEAKER ONE: Yes, you do.

SPEAKER TWO: No, I don't.

SPEAKER ONE: Great.

SPEAKER TWO: Now what?

SPEAKER ONE: Come here.

SPEAKER TWO: Come here?

SPEAKER ONE: You want a hug, don't you?

SPEAKER TWO: We're going to die, be sucked up, blown to smithereens. What's the use?

SPEAKER ONE: I think the wind is dying down. Drive!

SPEAKER TWO: The calm before the storm. Positive thinking. At least I like you for that.

SPEAKER ONE: I wish Grandmother was still alive. She just left us.

SPEAKER TWO: Shut up about that. Just shut the hell up!

SPEAKER ONE: She'd say, "Just keep on keepin' on."

SPEAKER TWO: Yeah. She would.

SCENE EIGHT

SPEAKER ONE: We have to stop meeting like this.

SPEAKER TWO: Are you wearing your mother's dress?

SPEAKER ONE: It's from the forties. I like it.

SPEAKER TWO: Why can't you just be yourself?

SPEAKER ONE: The shoes go nicely too, don't they?

SPEAKER TWO: Am I singing Dixie over here?

SPEAKER ONE: I was born in the wrong era.

SPEAKER TWO: I really want to slap you right now.

SPEAKER ONE: What did you say?

SPEAKER TWO: Hard.

SPEAKER ONE: Why are you so angry all the time?

SPEAKER TWO: I'm not what you'd call angry. Not really.

SPEAKER ONE: I'd say you were. Anyway, I think I look foxy.

SPEAKER TWO: Are you joking with that word?

SPEAKER ONE: Foxy, foxy, foxy. So there.

SPEAKER TWO: I'm out of here.

SPEAKER ONE: We've got to stop meeting like this.

SPEAKER TWO: Hey! Where do we meet next?

SCENE NINE

SHE: Let me get this straight. You want all Mother's jewelry?

HE: She promised it to me.

SHE: You don't even have a girlfriend.

HE: You don't know that.

SHE: You tell me everything. You never mentioned a girlfriend.

HE: It's mine and I'm taking it.

SHE: Stop it.

HE: You'd better leave.

SHE: AHH! You scratched me. Damn you.

HE: Is it bleeding?

SHE: You'd better call 911.

HE: You're not calling anyone, missy.

SHE: You are acting so weird.

HE: I'm going to pretend I didn't hear you say that.

SHE: No! Not that one. That one is special. She promised it to me.

HE: Mom's pet to the end.

SHE: Oh, little Tommy got his feelings hurt. Boo-hoo.

HE: That scratch is just the beginning.

SHE: Okay, okay. Here.

HE: All of it?

SHE: If it means that much to you.

HE: I have my own reasons.

SCENE TEN

HE: I'm being transferred.

SHE: Yes.

HE: Did you hear me?

SHE: I think I'll have some ice cream. Do we have any butter pecan?

HE: Butter Pecan?

SHE: Yes, I love the nuts. Crunchy.

HE: Forget it.

SHE: The ice cream?

HE: Us.

SHE: Oh, that.

HE: Yes.

SHE: That.

HE: There's some vanilla. Don't eat it all.

SHE: I always save something for you.

HE: Really, who'd have guessed it?

SHE: Whom indeed?

HE: Are you coming with me?

SHE: Are you going without me?

SCENE ELEVEN

SPEAKER ONE: Hi.

SPEAKER TWO: Go away.

SPEAKER ONE: I don't like you.

SPEAKER TWO: That's mean.

SPEAKER ONE: You meaner than I am.

SPEAKER TWO: I'm a butterfly, the color prism.

SPEAKER ONE: You are making no sense. Are you on something?

SPEAKER TWO: My dopamines are doing double time.

SPEAKER ONE: You're high as a kite.

SPEAKER TWO: Don't take it so personally.

SPEAKER ONE: I'm not; it's just that I thought you wanted off the stuff.

SPEAKER TWO: You want some, and you know it.

SPEAKER ONE: You don't know anything about me. God, you look like hell.

SPEAKER TWO: Been there and back, so what's the diff?

SPEAKER ONE: Let's get Sammy to help us.

SPEAKER TWO: Why is Sammy always the great one, the one with the answers?

SPEAKER ONE: Because he's been through this before.

SPEAKER TWO: I don't want him to know this time.

SPEAKER ONE: I can't take you anymore. You're throwing your life away.

SPEAKER TWO: It's my life.

SPEAKER ONE: So throw it away.

SCENE TWELVE

SPEAKER ONE: I know what that means.

SPEAKER TWO: What - - WHAT means?

SPEAKER ONE: When you answer a question with a question.

SPEAKER TWO: One psychology class, and you think you're Freud.

SPEAKER ONE: You've always been jealous.

SPEAKER TWO: You've got to be joking.

SPEAKER ONE: What's the joke?

SPEAKER TWO: I guess it's always on me.

SPEAKER ONE: I'm trying to think of another question.

SPEAKER TWO: You drive me mad.

SPEAKER ONE: You know what makes me tick, and I know - -

SPEAKER TWO: What makes you tick...

SPEAKER ONE: Tick. Tick. Tick.

SCENE THIRTEEN

SPEAKER ONE: Drat! You know my plan.

SPEAKER TWO: You're evil, and I can't trust you.

SPEAKER ONE: Did you think I really could be trusted?

SPEAKER TWO: I, oh, so hoped so, and yet - -

SPEAKER ONE: Yeesssss…go on, my pretty

SPEAKER TWO: I feel uncomfortable when you, when you - -

SPEAKER ONE: Stop this unyielding nonsense, come to me NOW !

SPEAKER TWO: You're hurting me, let go, I say, let go!

SPEAKER ONE: NEVER!!

SPEAKER TWO: It's always been you, hasn't it, lurking behind the curtains.

SPEAKER ONE: Not anymore! I stole the curtains!!

SPEAKER TWO: Beast! Animal! Thief!

SPEAKER ONE: And I'll steal your heart, if only you'd give me a chance.

SPEAKER TWO: My heart is locked in a box.

SPEAKER ONE: Aha! So you do have a treasure. My plan is working!

SPEAKER TWO: I'm lost.

SPEAKER ONE: You were lost the day you chose him.

SPEAKER TWO: I could tear my hair out.

SPEAKER ONE: No! I'll sell it and make a fortune.

SPEAKER TWO: Then I'll burn this house down!

SPEAKER ONE: Well, my little firefly, I'll hose you down with kisses!

SPEAKER TWO: Aaaahhhh!!

SCENE FOURTEEN

SPEAKER ONE: Where is the checkbook?

SPEAKER TWO: I don't know.

SPEAKER ONE: Well, didn't you have it last?

SPEAKER TWO: I thought we'd agreed - - that I have a job now

SPEAKER ONE: Do you have it or not?

SPEAKER TWO: Yes.

SPEAKER ONE: Give it to me.

SPEAKER TWO: Why?

SPEAKER ONE: Because I have to pay the bills.

SPEAKER TWO: I spent some.

SPEAKER ONE: How much?

SPEAKER TWO: I have a job now.

SPEAKER ONE: Yes.

SPEAKER TWO: I contribute.

SPEAKER ONE: Finally. Give it to me.

SPEAKER TWO: I'm disconnecting, I'm disconnecting, I'm disconn - -

SPEAKER ONE: - - Give it to me.

SPEAKER TWO: Here.

SCENE FIFTEEN

SPEAKER ONE: Oh…hello…see you're still here

SPEAKER TWO: Yes.

SPEAKER ONE: Did you kiss me?

SPEAKER TWO: I believe we kissed.

SPEAKER ONE: Oh. Where am I - - exactly?

SPEAKER TWO: How could you forget?

SPEAKER ONE: I'm not sure. It all went black.

SPEAKER TWO: Do you remember anything about it?

SPEAKER ONE: I still have sensations.

SPEAKER TWO: I still have thoughts, lots of great images.

SPEAKER ONE: My intuition says - -

SPEAKER TWO: My heart says - -

SPEAKER ONE: That it was interesting.

SPEAKER TWO: That it was quite pleasant.

SPEAKER ONE: Oh. Is that what you're remembering?

SPEAKER TWO: That it, whatever - - was something we can discuss openly.

SPEAKER ONE: Like adults, calmly, bit by bit.

SPEAKER TWO: Things have changed now.

SPEAKER ONE: I'm afraid. I should go.

SPEAKER TWO: I'm afraid too, but you need to stay.

Pause.

SPEAKER ONE: Okay.

SCENE SIXTEEN

SPEAKER ONE: Why do you always move away?

SPEAKER TWO: Because I'm like our universe, I'm not static.

SPEAKER ONE: I agree. You are in constant movement.

SPEAKER TWO: Oh, do my ripples affect you at all?

SPEAKER ONE: You do have more *red* coming from you than any other color.

SPEAKER TWO: Ooh...you're wearing your physicist hat.

SPEAKER ONE: Why didn't you visit me?

SPEAKER TWO: I lost my keys. Couldn't drive...

SPEAKER ONE: With the rhinestone key chain I gave you?

SPEAKER TWO: I guess the dark matter sucked it up.

SPEAKER ONE: You are my dark matter.

SPEAKER TWO: Does that make you my light?

SPEAKER ONE: We need each other. Don't fight it.

SPEAKER TWO: Like the infinite universe, you are my constant noise.

SPEAKER ONE: You love it.

SPEAKER TWO: The big - -

SPEAKER ONE: Bang!

ABOUT THE AUTHOR

Janice Fronczak is an actress, director, drama therapist and playwright. A tenured Associate Professor of Theatre at the University of Nebraska at Kearney, she teaches acting and playwriting and directs main stage productions. Fronczak has directed and taught at various summer stock theatres such as the Center for Cultural Arts (COCA) in St. Louis, University of Alaska Theatre for Young People (Anchorage), Theatre West, Brownville Village Theatre and the Blackhills Playhouse. She won a Directing Fellowship from the Kennedy Center American College Theatre Festival (KCACTF) in 2003, is a theatre respondent for Region V KCACTF-member university theatre productions and was awarded the Mentor award from the UNK College of Fine Arts and Humanities in 2009.

Fronczak started writing twelve years ago as a result of her desire to find new and accessible monologues and scenes for her beginning and intermediate acting students of all ages and skill levels. Throughout that time, she obtained her MFA in Theatre Pedagogy from Virginia Commonwealth University in Richmond, Virginia, started three separate theatre programs, including one at a women's medium security prison, had eight of her short ten-minute plays published by Heuer Publishing, became a certified feng shui consultant and started work towards becoming a Registered Drama Therapist. Along with these unique life adventures, Fronczak soaked up every off-the-beaten-path unexpected chance meeting or quirky, memorable character to put into her mental file to show up later in her writing. Her full-length play, *Corn Man* is slated to have its premiere production at the University of Nebraska at Kearney in Fall 2010. Fronczak has two screenplays, *Adagio 3* and *Galveston* to her credit, waiting to be picked up by a lucky production company. Her latest attention has been rounding up her twelve-year collection of original monologues and formless scenes, entitled *Blue Food*, to offer to the theatre world.

CPSIA information can be obtained
at www.ICGtesting.com
Printed in the USA
FFOW02n0939060118
44365322-44054FF

9 781615 882014